MY BEST LOVED STICKS

MY BEST LOVED STICKS

by *Freda*

Photographs by

Oscar Hedlund

Arlington Books
King St, St James's
London

MY BEST LOVED STICKS

First published in paperback 1989 by
Arlington Books (Publishers) Ltd
15-17 King Street, St James's
London SW1

First published in Great Britain 1984 by
Arlington Books (Publishers) Ltd

Originally published in Swedish 1983 as
Mina Bästa Pinnar
by Skogs Boktryckeri AB, Trelleborg

© *Oscar Hedlund 1983*
Translation © *Joan Tate 1984*

Printed and bound in Great Britain by
Billing & Sons Ltd, Worcester

ISBN 0 85140 771 4

CONTENTS

The author, Freda, and her friend, Pippa with their
photographer and master, Oscar Hedlund.

Foreword

One of the tragedies of my childhood was when our Springer Spaniel, Freckles, was run over, shooting out of the front gate into the path of a passing American tank. Fortunately our desolation was tempered next day, when a friend brought us a golden retriever puppy. We called him Simmy. He was the runt of the litter, and arrived with a broken paw encased in plaster. He quickly established himself as a tremendous character, stealing our hearts and commandeering all our sofas and beds.

When we moved after the war to Ilkley, on the edge of the Yorkshire moors, Simmy discovered the opposite sex, and would spend hours, even days, out on the razzle. Often exhausted, he would fall asleep in the middle of Ilkley High Street, and unlike the ill-fated Freckles, the traffic just drove round him. His favourite haunt was the local cinema where he fell in love with the lady projectionist. Time and again we received telephone calls complaining that she was having difficulty changing the reels, because Simmy insisted on sitting adoringly at her feet, shaking paws with her.

On another occasion he disappeared for several days. Distraught, we combed the neighbourhood, questioning farmers, keepers and shepherds. Then one morning I noticed Simmy cheerfully sauntering down Ilkley High Street leading a small scruffy boy on the end of a piece of string. On seeing me a flicker of embarrassment appeared on Simmy's face, before he bounced up with every show of delighted surprise.

"Simmy," I cried joyfully, flinging my arms around his neck. "That's not Simmy," said the boy in outraged tones. "That's Rex Booth."

Simmy had stayed with them for so long, they had evidently given him a new name, and even gone to the police making an application to adopt him. Fortunately the required week hadn't run out, and Simmy was returned to his rightful owners.

Much of my time was spent hawking the long suffering dog round local dog shows. He never won anything, except fourth prize once when there were only four dogs in the class, and he loathed every minute of it, particularly the baths beforehand. To avenge himself, he invariably escaped during the show and had to be paged over the loud speaker: "Will the owner of dog No . . . currently demolishing the Fancy Gateaux stall . . ."

My abiding memory however was seeing him cantering up the drive, aware that he had played truant too long. Like an erring husband, who after an amorous lunch with his secretary, brings home guilt presents for his wife, Simmy would be searching round for a dead leaf, or a stick or an ancient bone to present us on arrival. When he died we were all heart broken.

It was the nudge of memory therefore that made me fall in love with Oscar Hedlund's photographs in this enchanting book. For here was Freda, his golden retriever, behaving just like Simmy, chasing sticks, collecting dead leaves, countering the effects of a soapy bath by immediately wallowing in the muddiest pool, reacting to dog friends, and above all, humouring the human race. Mr Hedlund has certainly produced the most touching photographs I have ever seen.

The text when I first saw the book was in Swedish and beyond me. Now it has been translated into English, and I cannot recommend the book too highly to anyone who wants not only a good laugh but also to get inside the mind of a dog.

The story consists principally of dialogues between the older, wiser and wittier Freda, the golden retriever, and an impulsive, inquisitive black Labrador puppy called Pippa. Freda is a kind of Barbara Woodhouse among dogs, who believes the human race is much happier if kept in order.

"We started taming people," she claims, "as long ago as the Stone Age." She gives helpful hints on coping with their chronic insecurity, their lust for power and their desperate need for love.

"Your human can be kept busy throwing sticks, and a small camera will also keep him out of mischief on walks. Or encourage athletic games, that make him feel close to Nature."

The book is also a gentle satire on Human Folly. "Nothing," says Freda sadly, "makes a dog feel so sick as those pills people give us against travel sickness." She muses on the difference between town and country, has a go at bureaucrats and town planners, and even wonders who licks the envelopes from the Inland Revenue. Her comments on other dogs are as funny as they are perceptive.

Freda, 9, and Pippa, nearly 2, give new meaning to the old art of conversation.

"The dog's one aim in life," wrote J.R. Ackerley, "is to bestow his heart." Many people abuse this love – often through ignorance. Oscar Hedlund's book should be read by everyone who owns, or who intends to own, a dog to give them an infinitely better understanding of the joys and responsibilities involved.

Jilly Cooper

About being young

My name is Freda and I am a dog; to be more accurate, a golden retriever. I am now ten years old and am entirely self-taught.

In moments of leisure, I have written this book. In some ways it is entirely about me, as that is a subject I know quite well. But I wish to share it. I feel a need to dig up what I have buried over the years.

Not least, I feel it my duty towards my young friend, Pippa. She is the youngest in our family, a bewilderingly lively labrador.

Pippa is never still. She always seems to be going somewhere. There is a glint of mischief and a real zest for life in her golden-brown eyes. Even the most obvious things in life manage to arouse her curiosity. Occasionally, even I am made speechless.

"This business of being young . . . what does it really mean?" Pippa asked me in her impulsive way.

At first, I fell silent in philosophical meditation. To be 'young' or 'old' in today's society is not simply a matter of age. It is bewilderment when faced with a feeling. But that was probably rather too difficult for a ten-month-old puppy to understand.

"Let's say the difference between you youngsters and us old is The Fence," I said, using a simile the young understand.

Life, like this book, begins at the beginning. What sooner or later looms up is some form of fence.

We puppies are not toys

At first, Pippa was rather troubled by the fence. It always seemed to be in the way when she wanted to get out into the world. I nodded in agreement.

"Well, Pippa, we all remember the fences of our childhood. Puppies have to stay behind the fence – all kinds of fences."

But puppies don't have to feel imprisoned behind them. On the contrary. A puppy can make its first great discovery in peace and quiet behind the fence all by itself.

Pippa looked thoughtful and I realized that I would have to tell her about when I was a puppy myself.

There were five of us in the litter. I don't think we gave much thought to the fence. I just remember filling the quiet countryside with noise and games all day long. Mother was called Lisa. She was a golden retriever, honey-gold, kind at heart but on the surface apparently quite stern. Of course, she had quite a job with us little mischiefs.

Lisa was very particular about one thing. Puppies were to help out and learn to behave as early as possible. She always stressed this in a most ingenious way. "Just enjoy yourselves," she would say lightly.

Then suddenly we didn't want to enjoy ourselves. Instead, we all set about doing useful little jobs like fetching sticks, for instance, and not peeing on the carpet, not biting the television cable and not crawling under the gate down by the road.

Carrying a small leaf, for instance, would do. The important thing was to carry something about with you.

"I like leaves, too," said Pippa eagerly. "They tickle your mouth."

We realised that all the fun and all those delicious smells were on the other side of the fence.

Pippa's mother is called Petra and she has the most beautiful eyes in the world. She also tells her young what it was like when she was a puppy.

"I always say, the most important thing is for puppies to find out that they're useful in some way, and that they aren't just there to loaf around and be lovely and cuddly . . ."

In the way that mothers have, we started discussing how one should bring up puppies.

"Restless young come from idle young," I said.

"You have to take them by the scruff of the neck sometimes," Petra said. "Carefully, of course."

Pippa grabbed a little leaf that would do perfectly well, but she was looking so thoughtful that I realised she was wondering what being a puppy really meant.

So wise old Petra also thought it best to tell her just what it was like: "Everyone has to be small before they're big. So you have to make sure you're just happy as you are. You don't have to try and make yourself as big as others. Make the most of it, Pippa, and enjoy being small. You'll be big soon enough. Then it's a question

of enjoying being big . . . life's roughly like that."

Pippa looked at her brother Charlie, one of the naughtiest puppies in the litter. Then she looked at me. "What a difference!" sighed Pippa. She immediately set about growing big.

Pippa soon found out what happens when a puppy tries to take a stick from a big dog.

"Now I'm going to teach you how to behave," I said with a terrible growling from the back of my throat.

"Behave?" hiccupped Pippa, backing away.

The 'behave game' is a useful game I learnt long ago from Mother Lisa. "This is only for your own good!" Mother Lisa used to growl when she gave us those little snarling warnings.

We puppies all thought it looked awful and used to squeal loudly. But it did look quite funny, too, so we used to think up lots of little pranks so that Lisa would wallop us and growl that it was 'only for your own good'.

I learnt the 'behave game' and then tried it out on Elaine, the

I thought it would be good for Pippa to join me sniffing around, as long as she kept in her place.

She behaved very well until we discovered an old stick, half-buried in the rubble of leaves.

It's only for your own good, I told her, as I explained just who should keep the stick.

terrier next door. First of all, I carefully noted exactly what Mother Lisa did – how she caught me, how she gently seized my puppy fat, how she pushed me over and what subdued roaring should sound like.

Then I was able to set upon little Elaine with some confidence. The moment I was nipped on the backside by fiery Elaine, I realised that I had made a big mistake. Being small is not just about size.

"A small four-year-old terrier can turn out to be terribly large," Mother Lisa consoled me.

There is also something peculiar called 'experience'. If you have some of that, you escape being walloped too many times. But she

ABOVE: *Elaine seemed just the right size to try it out on . . . but Elaine was larger than she looked!*

thought she could wait a while before starting to explain that to all of us.

We preferred to spend our time playing quiet games with nice sticks, to trying to get fiery Elaine to behave.

But one serious problem always arose – which of all those sticks should you choose?

"Search around and find a stick that's *just right*," Mother Lisa said.

"Just right?" we whimpered, finding a tiny little stick and then a huge great stick.

Pippa sighed and exclaimed that Life was certainly not easy.

"I expect I'll spend the rest of my life looking for a stick that's just right," said Pippa in a dignified, but rather woebegone way.

For it's true, every stick involves making a choice, making up your mind, it's exciting, it's worrying. . . . "Sticks can make the

OPPOSITE: *Mother Lisa's grip is still fresh in my memory.*

21

nicest puppy mean, and even very nasty, if it wants to be. But sticks can also bring out something good in a puppy: joy, generosity . . . I remember what happened to Boy.''

Mother always acquired a mild glow round her melancholy grey nose at the memory of Boy. He was one of my brothers, perhaps the nicest of them all. I always took his best sticks. "It doesn't matter,'' Boy used to say. "You take it, Freda, as long as it makes you happy . . .''

He disappeared north later on and found a good home with a plumber. They say Boy has never really liked sticks since, but prefers chewing the plumber's socks.

An important event in every puppy's life is The First Prank. A 'prank' is not really the same as 'mischief'. A prank is more exciting, almost dangerous. Mischief mostly gives rise to 'ooh' or 'naughty-naughty' from master or mistress.

A prank on the other hand, may lead to a slap on the backside! Or at the very least an 'Uggghhh!'

"That slap always comes sooner or later," I tried to say in a

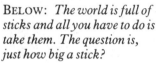

BELOW: *The world is full of sticks and all you have to do is take them. The question is, just how big a stick?*

ABOVE: *I got busy very early on with sticks and chewed them, if not for hours, at least for minutes. The best ones were delicious.*

joking yet foreboding manner. Pippa shuddered, realizing something nasty was coming.

"Before I tell you about this, you must first understand that neither 'prank' nor 'mischief' are nasty, nor meant to do any harm. You get involved in them from ignorance and usually when you're young, like you Pippa . . ."

But there are some who get up to this kind of mischief all their lives.

I have to close my eyes when I think of the awful memory of my first prank.

I can still see in front of me a very clear picture of a red-faced and furious master.

Most of all, I see the master's very best summer shoes, the left one to be exact. "It happened to get caught," I said simply. "Caught between my small puppy teeth."

The hairs on Pippa's back rose slightly she thought it so awful.

"It happened in the hall, right at the very back under the shoe-rack. There they were, those shoes. Their expensive scent was so tantalising and the exquisite leather gave such a wonderful hold for my small sharp teeth."

A shoe that's made of thin leather and is beautifully plaited can really give a puppy a great deal of fun – the joy of chewing! In the faint light of the hall, with its peace and quiet, as a little puppy, I really enjoyed that shoe, nibbling it bit by bit. What was left of it I kindly took into the master, who was sitting half-asleep in his television corner. I always wanted to share the good things that happened to me.

"My shoes . . . Help!!! My God, what have you done to my shoes, Freda?"

The master was shaking and rattling all over. I haven't seen him so upset and unbalanced since the television went off in the middle of *Dallas*. His voice sounded furious, but desperate as well.

"Oh, surely a pair of shoes isn't the end of the world," said the mistress.

"But those shoes are my best . . . damned dog!" sulked the

While the master ranted on about his shoe, I went into the woods to think the matter over.

master. And he sulked all evening.

Much later, I was to understand that expensive summer shoes don't just give pleasure to people. They also bring with them a whole load of worries – that the shoes will split, get lost, wear out, be eaten. Just like everything else people worry about . . . colour televisions, their stereo, cameras, cars, *things*! They buy a whole lot of nice things supposedly to satisfy and calm themselves.

Pippa asked what expensive summer shoes really tasted like.

"Like a real prank," I said sternly. "Very sweet at first. Then your backside hurts, after the walloping."

"There's another thing puppies ought to know. Not just puppies, for that matter . . . It's something everyone should know," I said in my teacher's voice. "Everyone should know his or her place."

Pippa ran off and stood a little way away. "Here? . . . Is this my place? I know it is," she suggested eagerly.

I just sighed, feeling an irresistible desire to yawn. So I yawned. Then I suppose I got that special expression wrinkling round my nose which means a lecture is coming: "My dear child, *to know your place* is not just knowing a special place. It's more a matter of finding your place in the great Reserve, knowing its scents, knowing how to behave, finding out about lots of things – briefly,

When dealing with youngsters, you have to take them seriously. They have to be allowed to face sensible opposition.

Here Pippa is meeting a little sensible opposition and it looks as if I am terribly angry.

Pippa's immediate reaction is to roll in self-defence.

it's a question of a *way of life*."

"Way of life?" echoed Pippa.

"For instance – keeping to your own sticks instead of pinching others!" I snapped. "It's not so much the stick as such . . . it's a question of your *respect* for *my* stick."

There was a bit of tail-down for a short time. Pippa has her own way of showing adults her respect. "I think I'll just lie on my back for a while," says Pippa.

It's good to take a rest now and again . . . but Pippa is quickly on her feet again. Life doesn't stop.

Talking about life and its wealth of wonderful opportunities – there's nothing in the world as lovely as puddles.

Water's alright. But it's better with mud in it. I suppose I must admit I spent most of my happy childhood lying in mud and puddles. Pippa also shows a tendency to be attracted to puddles, the muckier the better.

You could say life goes from puddle to puddle. The muddy puddles of experience. In them you find aroma, sweetness and everything that gives true flavour to your life. I think I'll have to

People have never really understood the charms of sticky mud and glorious big puddles.

Ugh . . . I hate bathtime!

read out a poem I once felt inside me in an incredibly mucky ditch.

If in your youth
You're in a muddle,
You'll never find
The ideal puddle.

Not a particularly long poem, but it's true. I have walked down a very long road. I started as a puppy and could hardly reach the mud. But in time, puppies grow bigger by the pound, by the inch and most of all in experience.

Then you find out about all the demands made on you. You discover the nasty things in life, like horrid tepid bathwater.

Pippa has her own way of approaching filthy ditches and revels in her mudbaths. The more mud the better, as far as she's concerned.

Pippa is a true labrador. She wholeheartedly believes in their traditional attitude to water.

Pippa actually has the remnants of webbed feet. She was born to leap into the nearest pool of water. She is 'water-retrieving', as it says in the dog hand-books.

"Don't let it go to your head, Pippa, but you do have a very impressive history," I say.

At it's simplest, it's rather like this: the cod-fishermen on the Labrador peninsula in North America needed an obedient, easily-trained and hard-working breed of dog that could help them in their work. Originally they all called the labrador "the little Newfoundland", as it was smaller than their local Newfoundland dog, but almost as patient and clever at jumping into the water, hauling on icy ropes or sledges or retrieving catches.

"So your coat's waterproof, Pippa. You'll cope with snow and cold as well as water, and your tail is rather like an otter's so you can steer magnificently through the whirlpools."

So Pippa is an excellent example of how well adapted the creatures are, that you find in the Reserve. Even Fritz, the neighbour's lazy dachshund, is particularly good at some things. Everyone has their own strengths and skills and we are all devoted to making the most of our opportunities. This is true even of old Butler, the basset hound, who in his muttering way gets others to do the work. Unfortunately, there are some who adopt this attitude from lack of understanding or sheer idleness . . .

Water is the most exciting thing in the world for the labrador, full of possibilities – and always wet.

A stone deer never moves, seldom says anything nasty, stays exactly where it is – just like some people.

Despite this fascinating discourse of mine, Pippa chose to get back into her own element with a splash.

Pippa plunges in and out, in and out. "Might as well keep on taking a dip, as I suppose we'll soon be sitting in front of the television, just like the master," she says. She seems to be getting to the rebellious age.

The strange thing is that people seem to have had wonderful times in pools only when they were young.

"*It was different in my day. Then you could always have fun,*" people often say, sinking back into their armchairs.

I raise my grey nose and wonder if Pippa has thought about something: "How do you know when someone's grown old?"

"They get a grey nose and a teacher-voice," giggled Pippa. For safety's sake, she immediately lies on her back.

"I mean, old in a *wrong* sort of way," I explain, lashing my tail impatiently. I get irritated in that sort of situation, waiting for an answer when I want to answer myself.

Age has nothing to do with 'getting old'. Everyone grows old sooner or later. You feel old when you start losing your curiosity and the excitement of discovery. Then you suddenly begin to find

They just make you want to yawn in boredom.

A nice basket rocked by the mistress provides a lovely, cosy life, but probably very boring in the long run.

that nothing's fun any more. Everything loses its smell. Scents and tracks lead nowhere.

Far too many people say lethargically that everything was more fun before, everything was better . . . *it was different in my day*. They're like petrified stone deer. Just like the one in the garden.

Once upon a time there was a small puppy who lived in a basket. It was warm and safe in the basket, the puppy thought. No strange nose poking over the edge, nothing dangerous even allowed to come anywhere near the basket.

So the little puppy thought it best to stay in the basket. She would stay there for the rest of her life. Even if it was dull and monotonous sometimes, she could at least remember that it was safe. You could say the poor puppy's life consisted of trying to fall asleep.

Suddenly a shadow fell over the basket. It had grown cold and rather nasty, the puppy thought. The sun had moved, and was now a little further away.

The puppy had a big think. She looked at the ground a bit

Light on one side, dark on the other, thinks the puppy faced with one of Life's mysteries.

I suppose it's a bit more frightening out in Life than in a basket.

further away, where the sun was playing. At first she tried to do exactly what she usually did – go to sleep. Then she did the only right thing.

The puppy leapt out of the basket, out into the sun, out into life.

The art of keeping your head above water

One Sunday in the middle of a marvellous summer, Pippa and I went down to the bay where we swim.

All the dogs in the district came, as most of them were free that day. The usual old gang was there, except Scariff the setter, who had squashed his tail in the door and wasn't supposed to get his bandage wet. Lucas the alsatian also had a genuine excuse, as he was going out with his master in the boat. And then Pompom the poodle, of course . . .

"He oughtn't to mix with 'a bunch of half-savage hooligans', as his master always says when we chew up those silly ribbons he has tied in his hair," Pippa said, grinning. So, no Pompom.

Instead there was a new little fellow trembling down on the beach. "Good-morning, I'm Flash," he said. Flash . . . *lightning*! Pippa started laughing so much that she got hiccups, but she meant no harm.

"Good-morning, little one," I said protectively, but Flash just looked miserable. All that wet stuff looked too awful for words.

The puppy wanted to swim, but didn't really know how to start. "You don't have to understand water . . . all you have to do is to get in and find out what happens afterwards," said Buster encouragingly.

They all started showering advice on the puppy. "Close your eyes and get in quickly," said Pippa, who always hurls herself straight into the nearest water.

"Backwards! Get in backwards, then you don't have to look at the awful stuff," said Fritz the dachshund, who likes standing on stones, and therefore takes a more academic attitude towards swimming.

"That's it, old boy . . . it's alright. I've got you," said his

It's not surprising that the spectators don't know who's going to get the wettest – Flash, learning to swim, or his mistress, trying hard to help.

It wasn't about the water or swimming . . . it was about daring to do something that looked dangerous, which Flash felt he had to do – despite the cocky Marco!

mistress, cunningly backing out of the water.

"What a fuss!" said Marco. He suggested that Flash should be thrown in. "Dogs are supposed to be able to swim long before they know how to." Typical Marco, being so tough on the poor little fellow. Flash almost started crying.

"Take no notice of him," said Buster, the Old English Sheepdog. "Marco's only that cocky when he's on land. When he's in the drink, you'll see, it's quite a different story then."

I told Pippa that Buster always talked sloppily like that because he's got a terribly grand pedigree with masses of champions in it. "It's just to call attention to that fine pedigree of his that Buster over-emphasizes a kind of dog simplicity," I explained. "You find the same thing in rich people who're ashamed of being rich."

Flash couldn't make it out at all, as he was much more worried about the water. Pippa sympathised, remembering how wet it was the first time she had gone swimming.

"Now everyone get out of the way," said Pippa. "Here's a lad

Flash didn't find Pippa's encouraging cries any help when he was going into the water for the first time. Nobody could help him – not even his persuasive mistress.

Marco behaved like every idiot father trying to make a 'man' out of a small boy.

going in for the first time, you know." Pippa is always saying that unnecessary 'you know', whenever she gets eager and rather bossy.

They all moved out of the way – except Marco. He started stamping and splashing and leaping round Flash and the water cascaded all over the place, the sun glittering in the drops. The terrific fuss and hullabaloo must have been heard miles away.

They were all barking at once suggesting how to help the new puppy take the plunge. Throw a ball? Chuck a stick? Mistress go first and tempt him in? Wet the puppy's stomach? His back? His nose?

They were all so busy helping Flash, they never even noticed what happened. Suddenly Flash grew tired of all the fuss. Calm and dignified, tail only slightly down, he walked straight into the

RIGHT: *All Flash's fears ran off him like the water. He was transformed.*

LEFT: *The transformed Flash, his seaman's eyes longingly on the horizons of the Great Adventure.*

water all by himself. When his paws no longer touched the bottom, then Flash knew he could swim.

When Flash started swiming it was rather worrying at first. He looked like a furious seal as the waves kept rolling over him and he stubbornly struggled up to the surface again. He looked a little foolish, too – a puppy with wild staring eyes, paddling away, tail straight out, puffing and blowing away like a grampus.

But he got better and better, calming down at each stroke. He was holding his nose high and steady, looking straight at us with a different and quite definite gleam in his eyes.

With his newly-found self confidence glowing like the drops of water in his coat, Flash came ashore and barked furiously at Marco. I talked to Pippa for a long time about this remarkable transformation. "Ultimately, it's not a question of keeping afloat. It's something called *self-confidence*."

Pippa eagerly agreed with this, because she remembered very

RIGHT: *Flash's first action was to bark at Marco, who was so astonished that he slunk off.*

clearly the time when her coat dried out for the first time.

You seem to be filled with warmth. You feel it running and rippling down your legs and it tickles a bit in your ears and there's a salty taste in your mouth . . . but in some way your eyes feel tremendously clear – *you can see things much more clearly*.

Self-confidence – there's nothing like it to make a dog's coat warm and dry. "As long as the others don't spoil it all," sighed Pippa. "The ones who don't understand a thing. The ones who keep interfering and deciding."

She knows how to do it, just like Flash did. All of them around him – but no one able to help. He had to get into the water all by himself and paddle along as best he could on his own. "It's really one of the greatest discoveries a puppy can make," said Pippa, who knows all about water.

That's right, no-one should force us into the water. Nor order us to swim. Nor decide how we should paddle. Nor make youngsters do lots of clever things.

I can't say it often enough that this is not *just* about being in the water, it's just the same on land. "Yes, if you others would get out of the way, we can manage our swimming on our own," Pippa said.

I feel I must quickly mention one of my nicest childhood memories. It's about the gate looking out onto the road.

I suddenly felt that the gate wasn't just a gate. It was temptation, adventure, excitement. I wanted to get out through the gate. I can still feel my heart thumping and the strange trembling that came over me that day.

Then I did what I wasn't really allowed to do. I went down to the gate on my own and stood there for a long time. Through the open ironwork I could smell strange scents coming from the big world beyond the gate. Scents of promise, adventure, life.

At first I was rather scared, quite weak in the paws, yes, even right down to the tip of my tail. It was a new and quite exciting feeling that kept me there looking out of the gate.

Every youngster knows the temptation of all those scents and promises quivering on the other side of gates and fences . . . you just have to get out.

"Freda, the day will come soon enough when you will find yourself on the other side of your childhood's gate," said Mother Lisa, standing quietly in the background. She was right. One day something strange and peculiar called 'people' came. Carefully, they carried me out through the gate, out into life.

People as companions

When Pippa, now a dashing labrador, was really small, she loved curling up between the paws of her idol. Her idol was me.

We used to have many peaceful conversations about one thing and another. "I think I'll tell you a little about this business of hands," I said one day.

"You mean paws, I suppose?" asked Pippa.

"No, I actually mean hands. People's paws are called hands. And you'll come across hands all your life, Pippa, so you might as well know what they're like now." So I told her all about hands.

While I was at it, I included a lot of other things about people. How they behave, all their little whims, their need for constant attention, the joys they bring as well as the troubles. "People as companions," I said, savouring that rather weak way of putting it.

"How do you find a really good person?" she asked looking pensive and rather serious. Even I don't know that.

Ever-curious, Pippa never stopped asking me questions about people and why they behave as they do. One of the few times she would listen attentively to me!

I was just minding my own business when suddenly a hand descended from above.

A scratching from above

It usually comes quite soundlessly from somewhere up above.

They creep up on you when you're least expecting it, mostly outside on small patches of grass or similar fairly large surfaces that puppies like staggering about on.

"Hullo, little-fella!" a voice suddenly roars from above, but you know it's not God. It's the master, or some total stranger to whom a puppy on the grass is something so irresistible, it has to be patted.

"Ah, bless it!" the more sensitive are apt to moan in a kind of swoon. But *little-fella* . . . not that I really know what that means, but I do know what *always* comes next.

It's a sort of tickling feeling, a scratching and poking, usually just behind the ears, but often on your stomach, too. Something called 'hands' have again patted a puppy.

I have to calm down Pippa, who is quivering, by assuring her that these patting hands are perfectly normal.

"You mean paws, I suppose?" repeats Pippa, now at the age when youth starts correcting adults.

"I mean *hands* . . . dogs, lions, rabbits, bears, tigers, and to some extent cats too, have paws. People have hands. They are astonishingly useful all-round tools . . . amazing, really, what people get up to with their hands."

You could say that there are hands all over the place these days. Anyhow, that's what it seems like. All dogs come across hands. "That's why it's so important, Pippa, that from the very start your attitude to hands is the right one."

The girl and her friend in the park seemed rather nice.

Her friend was as careful as I was, so we had something in common.

Her hands were very soft and gentle, though rather hesitant at first.

Some hands like taking an 'Ugh' attitude, which we mostly try to ignore.

I'll tell you how my attitude to hands came to be the right one. It was dusk in the park. At first I noticed a kind of sweeping movement, a kind of white flash.

It was a young girl, with blond hair and a happy smile. Her hands were gentle and infinitely careful. I literally shivered with delight. But I also sensed that not all hands were that soft and kind.

That must have been the first time I really gave some thought to this whole question of hands. I thought all through my twenty-third week, and by week twenty-four I had acquired a general basic view of hands.

I had already discovered hard, firm hands and that these hands could also be kind, but in a different way.

So kindness didn't have to be soft and gentle. You could say that this is the most remarkable thing about people and their hands.

Pippa now has quite a clear picture of the fact that hands are different. Big hands, small hands, gentle hands and hard hands with calloused palms.

"As well as that, you'll find all hands have different ways of

53

patting us, holding us, being nice to us, but also, I'm sorry to have to tell you, being nasty to us. But all that will gradually fall into place, you'll soon discover."

Hands can be felt distinctly. Much more distinctly than people think. Every scratch behind the ear, the slightest tickle of the stomach . . . we dogs immediately know what kind of people there are at the other end of those hands.

The fact is, by nature I am slightly shy, well, almost reserved, they say. Because of this, I have acquired over the years, a good inventory of all the kinds of hands in the dog-patting trade. I would like to stress that hands should never be treated in an offhand way.

Pippa isn't quite old enough to understand such things yet, but she wags her tail attentively anyway.

There is one thing people really don't understand. They keep holding out their hands, often invitingly, but also abruptly, as if they had flung them out.

Most dogs take a guarded attitude at first. Then people think there's something wrong with the dog.

Some hands pat nervously and as far back as they can get. Others scratch with a good hard hand.

I soon found out that hands felt different although really they all look rather alike.

"Look – the dog's hopeless, a weak character." I've often heard that. But we have to catch the scent of their hands first, before we get involved in patting and can start becoming attached to them.

Hands tell you everything. They don't have to be gentle. They don't have to be 'used to' animals at all. All they need is to be honest.

"You should know, Pippa, that the gentleness of hands has nothing to do with actual patting. You should look at the twinkle in people's eyes and at the lines around their mouths."

When you're young, you usually prefer gentle hands, but gentle in a firm and 'practised' way. As you get older, that becomes rather unexciting . . . pat-pat usually. Then you start discovering new and interesting combinations.

I think I like kind eyes and awkward hands best. Children's
hands aren't the gentlest, no, indeed, often the opposite . . . and
they're not as confident as adult hands. But you can't help liking
them, with their happy energetic caresses.

So you see, I can feel something gentle and kind in an eagerly
thumping child, even if I sometimes prefer to retreat out of reach.

Patting dogs is a very common phenomenon. However, there
are some situations which always make me feel very uneasy. On
the surface, they may seem quite idyllic – a nice dog tied up
outside a shop, for instance, staring into the shop in that touching

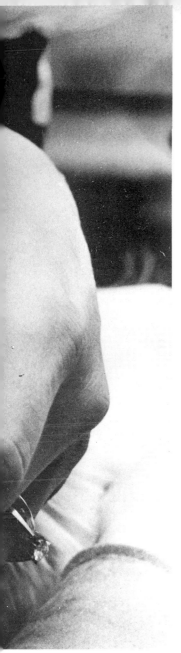

way, wondering when his master or mistress is coming back.

Then along comes a mother and her small child. Or it might well be a father with the same small child. The child catches sight of the dog.

"*Want to pat doggie!*" says the child firmly. Nearly everyone thinks that's nice and thoughtful. Except the dog. The dog strains on the leash, staring straight at the child, its upper lip twitching – if it's a fierce dog.

Usually it isn't fierce. It is much more likely to be a reserved, even frightened, dog. It is also tied up. Being tied up increases the feeling of your retreat being cut off and of not being able to move away. The dog starts tugging and pulling at the leash. He may feel threatened even though it's just a small child wanting to pat him. Dogs may bite then.

"What luck the child's mother or father was around . . . they're always so sensible," exclaims Pippa with relief. Pippa is young and credulous. She has her life before her. I don't wish to put a damper on her naive charm.

But I have to tell her that parents can be the most senseless and idiotic of the lot, especially when faced with strange tied-up dogs.

Just guess what happens next? The child is approaching this scared and incensed dog. The mother resolutely takes the child's hand, leading it even closer to the dog and saying: "Now don't hit the doggie, just *pat* it, *pat* it *gently*, darling."

The only reason that child still has its fingers is that the scared dog's master came rushing out of the shop, from where he'd seen what was happening.

"Keep your child away from the dog!" he cries.

"He only wants to pat it," says the mother.

"The dog's not used to children and doesn't like being patted by strangers. You should teach your child to keep away from strange dogs!" says the master.

Is the mother grateful for this resolute intervention? Do her eyes fill with tears of relief that all is well with her child and the dog?

OVERLEAF: *Soft hands invite a relaxed attitude, but a certain watchfulness should be maintained.*

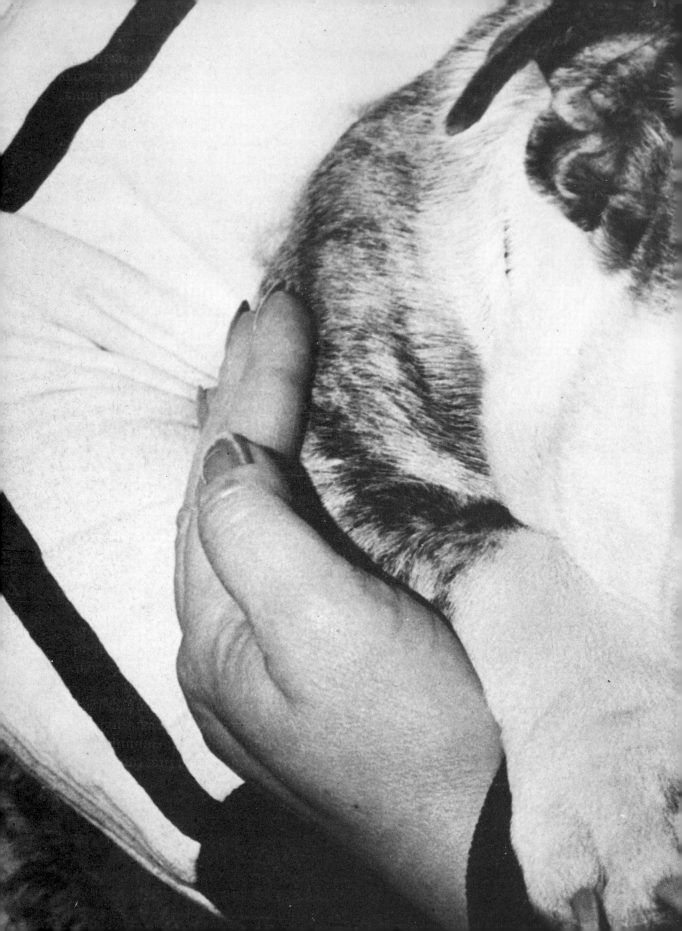

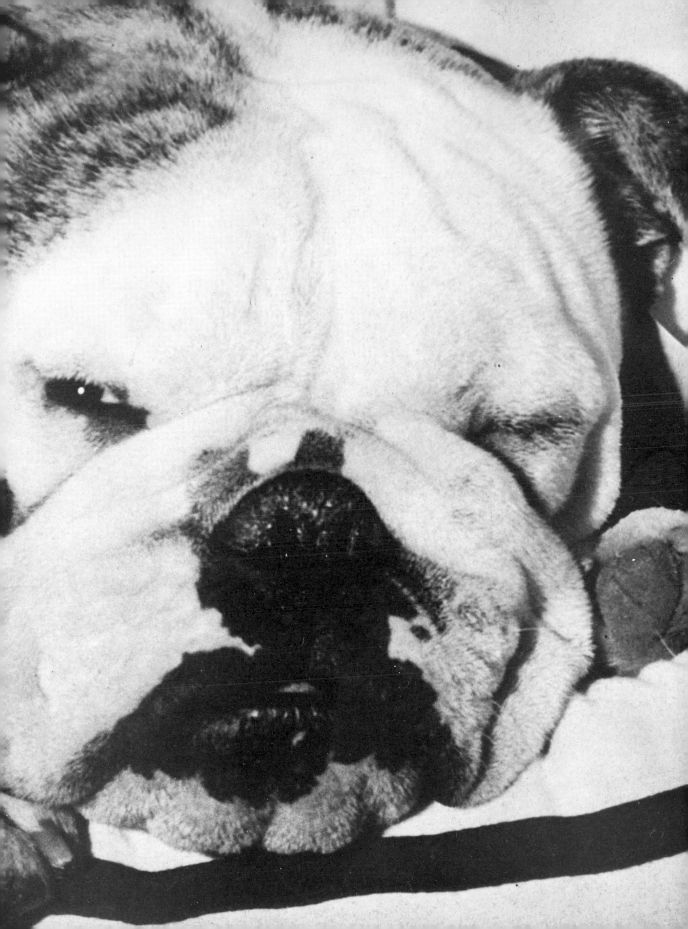

ABOVE: *Children's hands
are awkward, but they can be
gentle if properly trained.*

OPPOSITE: *It must be
something about the actual
patting, as paws just don't
feel the same as hands.*

No. At first she was angry, then furious, shouting at the owner
to "keep your damned mongrel indoors instead of letting it
frighten children!" She also screams that dogs that don't let
anyone pat them are sick dogs and should be shot on the spot.

Pippa is so upset now, her back hairs are standing on end.
"ANGRY DOG BITES NICE CHILD – that's what it will say in
the paper, isn't it?" she asks.

The best hands lift you confidently so that you feel safe and secure.

But mostly hands are marvellous. They support you and lift you up. All your worries disappear, and you think there's something awfully nice about people.

Some hands stroke you and some smack you. The difficulty is that you never know the difference beforehand. Some puppies have the misfortune to come across hard hands, and what is worse, unjust hands – they're the puppies who grow into angry dogs that bite. And all their lives, they shy away from being stroked. You should be sorry for that kind of dog. Sometimes, I think it's the same with people.

"How do people know when they should pat us?"

It's not easy to find a simple answer to that question. But if a person ever asked me, I would say this: it's an emotional matter. Suddenly there's a warmth inside you. You may even feel your eyes watering. Maybe you smile, almost without cause . . . and the hand tingles. Then there's really only one thing to do. Pat what you want to pat.

But a last word of warning, you must beware of unfriendly hands. People who don't like animals rarely admit it. They just bash us, without warning. Those are horrible, cruel hands. You can never trust them, even when they try stroking you. Then they're showing off and are lying.

It takes a long time to know their scent. But we never get used to that kind of hand.

At first people's noses feel funny, soft alright, but not really cold and wet.

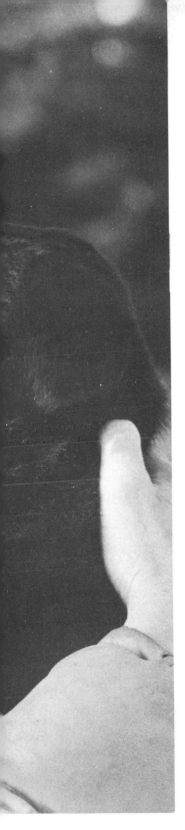

How do you find a really good person?

You've probably already decided to try and find someone as a companion. You think it'd be good with a small expectant nose snuffling at your ear and a soft whisper explaining what fun you are going to have together.

But I really must ask you, Pippa, whether you have truly considered what it means to be responsible for a person? Will you really be able to cope with a lively master and mistress?

You mustn't think I'm being discouraging with this rather down-to-earth talk. But I have to tell you exactly what it's like.

Basically, people are really quite nice. Especially at first, they're almost irresistible when leaning over the basket of puppies and literally swamping you with all kinds of compliments and nice remarks.

They seem to be clever, but you'll soon find out there's something large and shapeless, even bulky about people. They take up a lot of room. They're all over the place. They can be heard everywhere. You'll find it difficult to get away from them, even for a short time. People dominate and rule.

But at the same time they're astonishingly adaptable. It is a question of bringing them up properly. They demand a tremendous amount of patience and work from you, Pippa. From the beginning of time, their task has been to throw sticks and balls for us, thus ensuring eternal friendship.

People take up a lot of space in our lives and hearts, Pippa. So from the very start, you have to treat them with love and firmness.

They must be kept busy. Don't ask too much of them – nor too little. People aren't loveable cuddly little creatures, they're very much alive.

So they need a firm paw for encouragement and guidance. Appeasing them and making few demands on them just makes them difficult, often exacting. It's easy to lose your temper with

RIGHT: *But you get used to all the fuss and attention after a while.*

LEFT: *They turn to us in a rather moving way, looking for affection.*

them. But you must try to remember – *they're just ordinary people.* Let them be people, too. All too often, we dogs have a tendency to 'doggify' people, so to speak, giving them qualities that are ours alone. That's when we ask too much of them, which makes them insecure and awkward, and often creates problems.

No, try to meet people on their own level instead. But remember, people are herd-animals, who don't always do what you or they want – but often do what others think. However strange it may seem, people do vary enormously.

ABOVE: *Winter as well as summer, people are totally absorbed by their hobbies – but leave them alone – it develops endurance . . .*

"Then how do you choose a really good person?"

"Well, now, Pippa, I wish I could answer that. I have to tell you that it really is a matter of chance, choosing a master and mistress. There are no easy-to-follow rules for choosing. Like Life itself, you have to carefully feel your way.

It's not as simple as many dogs think. You can't expect to find fully-guaranteed good, nice people by just judging from their pedigree, standard of living, social status or from whether they own a car, a boat or a big house.

No, you have to abandon such primitive criteria, Pippa. You have to rely on your instinct, your own sensitivity and feelings."

Let me explain more fully. I know perfectly well where my own sure eye for people comes from. The memory remains very clearly in my mind. It was a bright autumn day, with a touch of destiny in the crisp fresh air.

A whole series of 'prospective people' came to my childhood home, with the intention of what was called 'getting a dog'. They got worse and worse . . . strange people who behaved very oddly when faced with us puppies.

"Do dogs really need all that exercise?" one asked.

"Do they mean a lot of work?" queried another.

"I suppose they're house-trained?" demanded a third, promptly calling attention to the way he valued his house and belongings.

The worst were the 'canine-experts'. One made nasty faces and clapped his hands. One was quite crazy and banged a spade into the ground. They said they were 'testing our characters'.

My character was the very worst. I crept right in under the sofa and was thus considered to be seriously mentally disturbed. So, I managed to avoid the worst doggie people in the world – the ones who think they know all about dogs.

Then two amateurs came along. She had long soft hair and said she was no expert, but she'd always liked animals. That was evident from the way she picked me up. He was a plump little fellow who immediately started chucking sticks, because he'd learnt from the television that dogs like sticks.

I preferred sitting on the girl's lap to tearing about after sticks. In the end, Mother Lisa took pity on me and sloped off to fetch the

BELOW: . . . and if not occupied with this harmless task, who knows what mischief they wouldn't get up to.

If nothing else works, try looking melancholy and they will soon start feeling guilty.

stick for him, looking supremely bored as only a golden retriever can.

His behaviour made me think that perhaps he had some guts, aptitude and instincts which could be developed in the form of play.

So I decided that these two 'amateurs' should be allowed to choose me as their dog.

The moment of farewell was slightly sentimental and peculiar. You know that gate I'm always talking about when reminiscing . . . it now closed behind me for ever. I was taken into town in a car that growled and rumbled all the way.

Talking about town. Which is best, town or country? You often hear dogs say: "I like people alright, but you should keep them in the country, not in the town."

People's yearning looks follow us dogs around, and we can draw the wrong conclusions from that, thinking they're always longing

The more there are of you, the more effective this is. No normal person can resist these attacks for long.

to be somewhere else, the town-dweller in the country, the country-dweller in the town. Why are people so dissatisfied?

But, of course, you can keep people in town. You get used to collective living after a while. But watch out that they don't become possessively territorial and start talking about 'my best sofa'' 'my refrigerator', and so on.

People, as well as dogs, seem to need constant supplies of food to cope with their physical exertions.

*Note the elegant pose Pippa adopts
while pleading for some cake.*

The feeling of being inadequate is very common, a sign of the times, you might say. People have made this into an unnecessary fear, and if anyone can exploit it, then their dogs can.

You can stare people into a state of total disintegration. (But a melancholy dog staring in that accusing way is probably just begging for something.)

You especially, Pippa . . . the sighing looks of labradors can really tug at the heart strings.

OPPOSITE: *For once, Patsy has decided that she will obey Mary.*

BELOW: *They are both very obstinate and stong-willed. Naturally this leads to endless tussles, as well as a very close friendship.*

Here is my clever friend Patsy again, a really sturdy walker called a clumber spaniel. For people, I think she's the ideal friend. Her phlegmatic nature combined with a down-to-earth approach makes her especially suitable to be on the end of a leash.

Everyone who has ever tried to get Patsy to go where she doesn't want to go understands this perfectly well. Instead, it is Patsy who pulls people where they want to go . . . it's an example of psychological sophistication and what politicians usually call flexible objectives.

But most of all, Patsy likes people. Especially her young mistress, Mary, who did actually once have a tendency to pull in

Very early on, Patsy learnt how to persuade Mary that the way Patsy was going was the way that Mary had intended all along.

her own direction. She was allowed to then.

"But you only need to give them enough rope, and they soon come back," advises Patsy. She believes in 'freedom through responsibility'. She often talks about 'relationships', 'dialogues' and 'frames of reference'.

She has talked like that ever since the co-existence course she went on to find out why people are as they are. "But we didn't get very far," she sighs.

'Is there really any evidence to show that people can think?' was the theme of the course. Although her mistress mistakenly thought that they were there so that Patsy would learn to obey such commands as 'Heel' and 'Sit'.

The course did get as far as various human types, though. They all agreed the worst are what are called 'aimless'. They're inconsiderate dog-owners. They let dogs bark at all times, mess the place up, jump up at people and in every way behave badly . . . Through lack of understanding, this has created a lot of dog-haters. "They should rightly be called dog-owner-haters," growls Patsy.

In some ways, I agree with her. But there's also a kind of dog-owner I personally find just as bad – the self-appointed canine-experts.

They're awful people who not only know everything, but also feel they have to tell you. The canine-experts push in everywhere, literally showering everyone with their nerve-racking 'expertise' that includes almost everything – from tartar and dandruff to questions of excrement 'from a policing perspective'.

Canine-experts never make good companions. They like neither dogs nor people.

Fetch the ball, master!

LEFT: *Sometimes I do show off when playing ball so that master can impress the other masters and mistresses in the park.*

The game I am trying to teach my master is great fun. An ordinary simple stick will do. Or something easy to throw that doesn't cost anything. In principle, all that's necessary is that it can be thrown.

I am trying to persuade the master away from his preposterous idea that the things that are most fun are expensive, shiny and preferably rather heavy, and also can only be found in special shops. We have the most fun of all with a small red ball.

The game goes like this. First the master takes the ball away from me. Then he throws it as far away as he can. That's not particularly far. But he does his best, anyhow, and at least that's a little way for me to run.

The central point of the game is that I shall run and fetch the ball, then put it down at his lord-and-master's feet. I do that

RIGHT: *Another of my favourite balls – fun to chew as well as to chase.*

time after time, and still enjoy it.

Then suddenly I can't find the ball. I just run around in confused circles, looking vaguely unhappy . . . but I'm only pretending. Out of the corner of my eye, I've seen where the ball is all the time. Guided as well, of course, by the typical master-scent that settles in a billowing cloud around the ball.

I give the game some educational content with this expression of pretended helplessness. The ball-throwing is elevated from empty, mechanical repetition to what you might call active master-training.

Let's see what really happens. I am running round and can't find the ball. "Fetch it! Fetch! Fetch! Not there, you idiot, no!" I hear the master yelling in his encouraging way.

The only way to silence him is either for me to fetch the ball, or for there to be other masters and mistresses around.

The latter causes a remarkable transformation. He is suddenly filled with the outdoor sportsman's patience and understanding of the complex problems involved in retrieval, adopting an objective attitude to the complications of finding the ball and encouraging me with quiet cries: "That's it, Freda. *Gooooood girl*, fetch the ball . . . fetch it! Clever dog, *there's* a clever dog," and so on and so forth.

At the same time he smiles with secret understanding at the spectators and says breezily: "Damn me, I do believe the fool's gone and lost the scent, tee-hee."

At which he strolls over to the ball and pokes at it nonchalantly with his foot, saying: "Here you are, old girl, here's your ball!"

Of course, I've known that all the time. However, I gaze at him with great interest until his trembling finger points at the ball.

"Now then! . . . Ball! . . . Fetch it!"

I don't. Not at that stage. Instead I sit down for a moment to weigh up the situation. Of course I can go and get the ball. I can catch the ball in flight whenever I want to, with great leaps that make my coat flare in the sunlight, all my inherited hunting instincts exploding and jaws greedily heading for the prey . . . much like when the master opens the refrigerator door for his evening snack.

Otherwise you can smell ball-scent everywhere. The whole of life is full of balls – and I've fetched them, one after the other, for sure. But I think the master himself should pick this ball up from the ground, seeing that he's managed to find it.

I'm not small-minded in my disobedience. I simply know it's important for the master to realise that he has managed to find the ball *all by himself*.

A master and his dog, according to the latest ideas of radical forms of co-operation, are seen as a small working-party. Outwardly, this seems both good and useful. But beneath the surface of a classic Master-Dog relationship, lies a deep chasm, a hair-raising injustice far beyond any elementary equality.

Let me give you a couple of examples. I am very quick. The master is not, except when he's running for a taxi. I have an extremely keen scent, while he can hardly find a hot-dog stall. I am not disparaging him. I'm just pointing out the widely different conditions that apply when people throw a ball for a dog.

Of course it's important people should feel they are participating and are being allowed to show their skills. But in the excitement of the game, they should neither be too stimulated, nor what is worse – mocked!

I am sure that it is when they feel their physical inferiority most that they fall back into their traditional lord-and-master ways.

"Freda. *Here*!" I can go there if necessary, because I'm going in that direction anyhow. But that doesn't substantially change anything. If I then seem to appear slightly crestfallen during that moment of slinking retrieval, it is because I am not in the least crestfallen. I am simply being thoughtful.

I am thinking about the master and how he loves playing ball. He is always so proud when he manages to find it. "Freda! Here it is, look . . . you nitwit!" he shouts affectionately.

I think the actual retrieval itself is almost beautiful – the master's head high, his proud strides, the ecstatic tremble in his voice as he tells the whole world: "Here it is, Freda!" Then he picks it up himself.

But then something amazing happens, an amusing bit of behaviour I don't think I'll ever really understand. *He throws the ball away again*! Again and again as soon as he's retrieved it, he throws the ball away.

All those 'musts'

The fact is they say I have 'hunting' in my blood. Not that I know what that entails, but you're supposed to follow your 'primaeval instincts' and then everything will be alright.

That simply means rushing out into the water and dragging ashore the nearest bird, I'm told.

But there must be some serious misunderstanding here. At least, that is what it seems like with all these birds. They just laugh at me when I make rather listless attempts to appease the master for the sake of some peace and quiet.

The master stands on the shore making a fearful fuss – begging, calling, insisting, almost threatening: "Freda – you *must*! You've got hunting in your blood. *All* golden retrievers have. You do nothing except fetch old birds. It's the Law of Nature, Freda . . . don't you feel it seething and bubbling in your blood?"

No. I can hardly feel the water. How could I possibly feel the 'predator in my soul' when the lake is full of nice ducks?

The master stands laughing on the shore. He's wearing his newly-acquired green shooting-jacket. The whole thing's just too awful for words.

Or else he's simply misread the instructions. He's got a dog-dictionary, in which it states quite clearly that 'the golden retriever has a good-natured and intelligent expression, enjoys the water and never minds retrieving even in winter conditions'.

"Read it for yourself, then," said the master ungraciously, last time we quarrelled.

I'll show the master something I think important.

I eased my way down into the water, fixed my good-natured look on a nice duck, and started feeling round inside me for those hunting-instincts. Not many there.

I do take a positive attitude to water –
but only when I am allowed to decide
for myself.

ABOVE: *Lakes should have enough space for everyone. I'm quite happy to share them with any number of ducks.*

"Swim faster!" shouted the master from the shore. The duck and her friends at once started swimming faster. I always swim at my usual pace.

But you can think when you're swimming after a duck. You can think about the Laws of Nature, for instance – incredibly foolish. They're the Laws of Man, aren't they, thought up to curb his sense of insecurity out of doors? The laws run on the principle that ducks always behave like ducks. And that all golden retrievers always chase ducks.

People can give us a lot of pleasure, with a sufficient balance between what is serious and what is fun in life.

As I said before, it's no use pretending it's not hard work, not just because of the extra trouble they cause.

They make the most amazing amount of mess. They need constant attention. They always want to be near us, they turn to us, constantly testing out the degree of our affection. I see no disadvantages in this – on the contrary. It is these qualities that make people suitable material for developing into pleasing and useful companions.

OPPOSITE: *The problem is the Law of Nature as written by the master. It says that I have to listen to the instincts within me and chase every duck as soon as I see it.*

RIGHT: *There always has to be a bit of give and take in any relationship.*

LEFT: *I think we started taming people as long ago as the Middle Stone Age (6000–1600BC).*

I shall show you how a good upbringing has already begun to show results.

The mistress and master are affectionate, well-adjusted, kind – what's usually known as 'good'. You don't make them into good companions like this by shouting and insisting, or by easily giving in to their little whims and caprices.

A kindly firmness forms the basis of all good upbringing. Few breeds show such multifold qualities as people do. Their inventiveness is unparallelled, their retrieving qualities astounding.

I never cease to be surprised by all the stuff the master brings home: colour televisions, digital toasters, quartz shoe-polishers, remote-control cleaning aids and so forth.

"Drop it!" I say sternly. Then he at once starts looking round for even more expensive and if possible even more unnecessary things. Oddly enough, he never buries any of them.

If only one could steer all that incredible energy, with its innate desire for material goods and territorial rights into something more

If properly looked after they can become very good companions. In fact our tastes are often remarkably alike.

positive and worthwhile.

As I see it, people have all the prerequisites for avoiding behaving as they do. They have poor scents, but nevertheless sniff their way through life. They're rather lazy, but clever at inventing labour-saving devices. And yet something's missing.

They say the mistress and I are rather alike. I take that as good, an observation from the heart. Then there's the question of who is like whom?

In town, we live in a rather drab red house. Opposite us was a grey house, but then the owners painted it white. Then suddenly our house became red in a pleasant, jolly way, suddenly gleaming. I think it's not only houses that take colour from each other. I think those of us who are together reflect each other, in the shadows as well as in the daylight.

That's the only reasonable explanation I have for the mistress and me growing alike. Animals adjust astonishingly well to people. If only it was the other way round a little more often.

The Great Reserve

Pippa is now old enough to know what I mean by 'The Great Reserve'.

"We all live in it, together with all the others," she says thoughtfully.

But she simply cannot know that all the others consist of about 850,000 different insects, 35,000 kinds of spiders, 20,000 fish, 8,600 types of bird, 3,200 mammals . . . of which only one kind is homo sapiens, people.

"They're fairly ordinary herd-animals," I say.

"How many of them in the herd?" asks Pippa.

"Well, I should think there are about 4.5 thousand million," I suggest, noticing at once that Pippa starts counting.

The Reserve is immense. But there are nevertheless worrying signs that it will not be large enough for us all. The Reserve is also a vast concept including everything that gives life to that huge herd.

"Security is a very common concept," I say. "It's what most of us try to find."

'Emotion' is another phenomenon that creates quite a stir. "There are a whole lot of different 'emotions', and yet most of them can be found in your small body as long as you have a large soul," I also say.

Pippa says nothing. She doesn't want to know any more at the moment. She puts her nose to the ground, sets off into the Reserve and at once finds tracks . . .

Look at all of it out there. It's mind-boggling, everything that exists in the Reserve.

Tracks

The Reserve is everywhere and nowhere. It is where you live your life. There are no fences there other than those you yourself put up. There are scents leading you to everything you dream about and hope for, but on the way there, you will be confused by other scents, the scents of reality.

The Reserve is indeed an amazing place. That is where we are all brought close to each other, and yet at the same time further away from each other.

Here we all are. All kinds of people, all kinds of animals. The Reserve was probably considered from the beginning to be sufficient for all of us, that its possibilities were unlimited, that its space could not be fenced in by horizons.

But unfortunately that wasn't so.

With 850,000 different species of insects, 35,000 species of spiders, 25,000 crustaceans, 20,000 fish, 6,000 reptiles, 8,600 birds and 3,200 mammals inside it – it's not surprising that people become nervous and spread out. In addition to that, dogs irritate people. Our toilet activities corrode their thrown-away beer cans and soil their broken empties. Space has become limited.

The Reserve is shrinking. Or maybe there are far too many of us – are we far too bulky?

People talk about a dog's sense of 'territory', not only a space to be in, scents to recognise, the herd to find your way to. It is something you have to fight for – but 'territory' has become more and more an expression for people's need to fight for their own conditions.

Does it show when I think? I often wonder whether people actually think. Maybe they just follow their instincts.

There seems to be less room in the Reserve, we are all hustled closer together . . . there aren't many wide open spaces left.

Two goldfish were staring at each other in a round bowl. They were thinking about one thing.

"If God doesn't exist, who gives us fresh water?" asked the more sensible one of them. That I think is a good way of indicating that there are things called people.

They are all over the place in the Reserve and there are lots of different kinds of them, but an 'average' kind of person has looked the same for between fifty and seventy-five thousand years. And now there are 4.5 thousand million of them in the herd.

There are tracks of them everywhere.

The tracks of the strongest are the most marked, the people destined to be successful. They just go straight ahead, seldom veering sideways, striding on and up.

I think it's more fun following hardly discernible tracks. They go through life with light, little steps, sometimes showing bewilderment, but also often courage. They lead you round in strange circles. They tickle my nose in a pleasant way.

They are the tracks of people who do not rush blindly straight at their chosen goals. The way there provides them with much more enjoyment.

One really should admit to one's dependence from the start. We are all dependent – on each other. That's how the Reserve was supposed to be from the beginning, anyhow.

Some people have a way of looking at you that could be called 'a dog-like look'. It's a sign of affection, the need for company, docility, love and similar states of weakness.

Now I'm being ironic, about the way people are. I mean that there's something good about being affectionate and having the ability to feel love.

They say we dogs don't have a sense of humour. We never understand jokes. We don't know any funny stories, either.

The only thing we can do is take people seriously.

When I indulge myself

I love doing something called 'indulging myself'. I just go around 'indulging myself', or rather with an old paper-bag containing the remnants of the heavenly smell of coconut and chocolate on my nose. It's a relatively inexpensive pleasure, and it's also low in calories. I feel slightly luxurious and more able to face life's less pleasing smells.

But people stare. "So you're going round with an old bag on your nose, are you, Freda? Ha-ha," laughs my observant master, and then starts making funny remarks about my behaviour not being quite 'normal'.

I admit that it's true that not all of us go around with paper-bags on our noses. But to label me 'abnormal' or 'peculiar', not to mention 'deviant', that really is taking things too far.

Everyone laughs and points, saying isn't she funny, our Freda! You just have to put up with it. A certain everyday courage is required from anyone brave enough to put an ordinary paper-bag on their nose in public.

The master is slightly ashamed of this paper-bag business. He thinks you shouldn't go around like that with a bag on your nose. If you like chocolate and coconut, then you should indulge discreetly, and not go around groaning ecstatically into old paper-bags.

"It looks as if you're one of those – er – lotus-eaters, Freda," says the master uneasily. "Irresponsible, a playgirl sticking her nose into the sweeter scents of life."

"You know how people talk," the master says furtively. That's

You can't even pick up a bag without attracting funny remarks from some people.

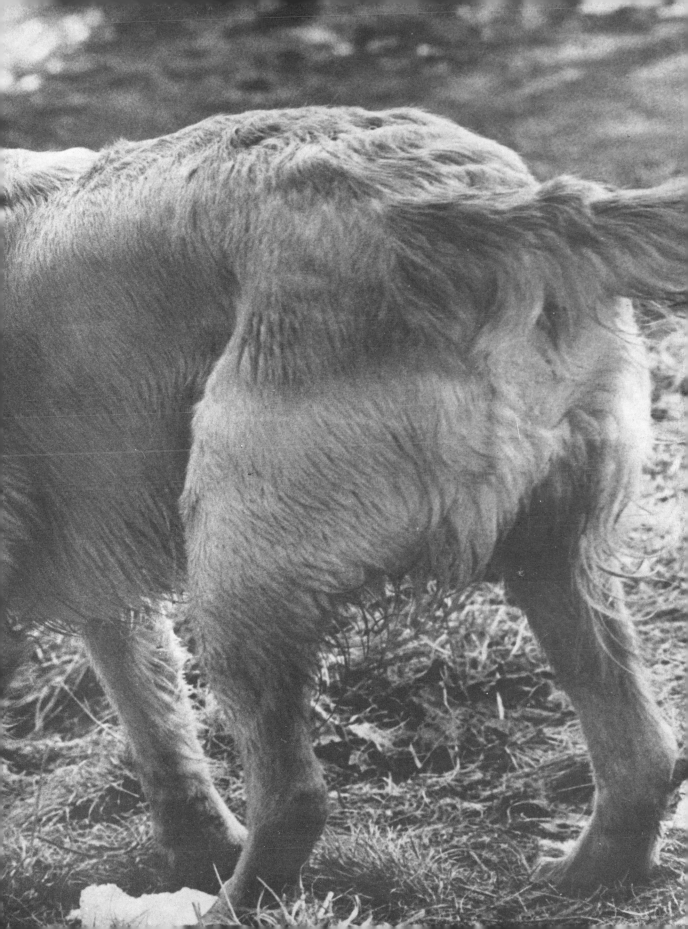

LEFT: *This is a very striking example of 'luxurious indulgence' – Pippa indulging in an old stick.*

RIGHT: *You may well wonder why Pippa enjoys that rotten old stick so much.*

LEFT: *It's not that particular stick, but that someone else wants to indulge in exactly the same stick . . .*

just how a typical secret-indulger talks! They indulge their pleasures in secret. They seem to follow two main principles: everything that tastes good is either bad for the teeth or is at least fattening; everything that's fun ought to involve an underlying sense of being either forbidden or at least some form of sacrifice.

For instance: "Darling, you've no idea what hard work it was, and all that food I had to stuff down in those terribly boring restaurants," the master usually says to calm the mistress on his return from those all-expenses-paid business trips.

The mistress says nothing, because she knows what he's going to say next: "But everyone goes to restaurants!" he says, excusing this fairly typical indulgence of his.

Indulgence seems to cause people unspeakable suffering.

Suddenly I find a ball. The stick is no longer the same. It dangles listlessly from Pippa's crestfallen mouth. She would rather indulge in my ball . . .

I think the main difference between us dogs and people is that we seldom dress up our indulgences in the virtues of labour. Anyone seeing Pippa indulging in a rotten old stick will understand what I mean! It is perfectly clear that her chewing of the stick is much more pleasurable than useful. She just eats up the stick, full stop.

Pippa seldom asks herself whether she is worthy of the stick or not. She just chews it.

My friend Butler the basset is muttering behind the fence. "Freda, you old moralist. Let people indulge in peace. I think it's good for the country's economy. Supposing everyone was content with an old paper-bag on his nose . . .?"

Butler is a real character. He stands soberly behind the slats, proclaiming his opinions on virtually everything.

Bessie, the white poodle, spends most of her time brushed and combed and feeling unsafe in her luxurious cage.

"The feeling of being imprisoned in some way will probably never go away," sighs Bessie. Nothing gives you such a suffocating sense of imprisonment as a safety-cage. Neither is it anything to do with the steel grid or the closeness of the bars.

"It's the actual feeling. You can actually be inside quite a small cage and regard everyone outside as locked up in an even smaller cage . . . provided you can escape the feeling of being shut in," I say philosophically.

Changes are very strange. At first, everything's new and exciting, but also alien and threatening. I don't really think anyone likes change because you never know what it's going to be like. The greatest change in my life came when I was suddenly shut up in a huge cage called Town.

110

I think Bessie's reached a difficult age. Or is her luxurious cage too small?

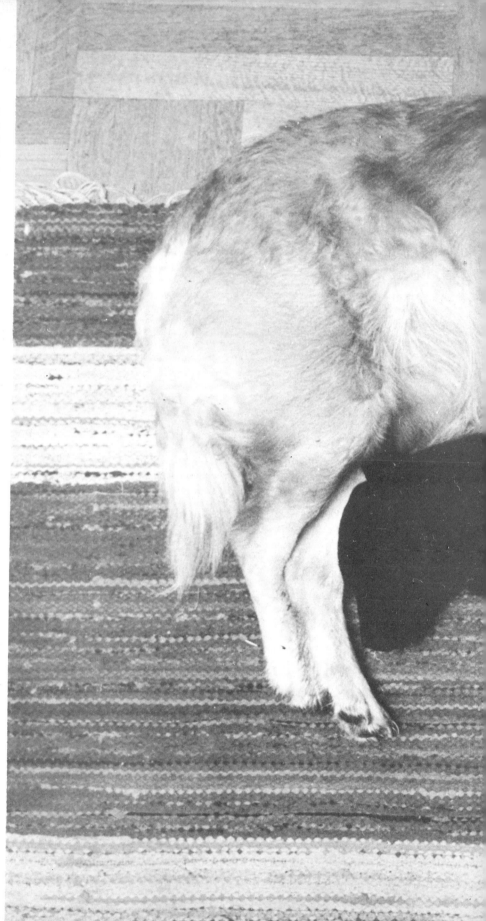

At first, Pippa was terribly afraid of me, but that soon passed. As soon as she was tired, she appointed me proxy-mother and promptly fell asleep.

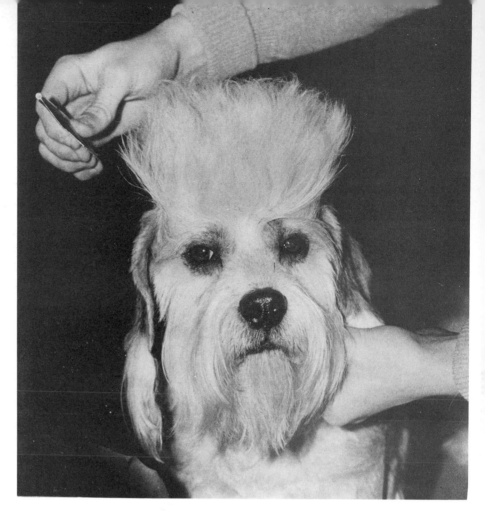

Some dogs are tidied and bullied into being the 'ideal dog' people long to have. Rather like the bright westie and his mistress at this show. A good demonstration of how people decide where we're to go, controlling us from tip to tail.

I think I was deeply shocked. It's a strain for a puppy to be moved from an idyllic home in the country to that strange and frightening corner of the Reserve called 'town'.

They let me out into a large cage called an 'apartment'. I kept slipping on the shiny floors. I chewed rugs that tasted of nothing but got stuck between my teeth. I got earache from the noise. My nose turned dry from the awful smell.

Then I did something terribly childish. *I decided that I wasn't going to like it.* At first it was easy not to like it and lie sulking in the dim hall. But it grew worse with time. The more I began to like it in town, the harder it became not to like it!

Very easily, so that I hardly noticed it myself, I started getting used to what had seemed nasty at first – a change. In fact, I began to like it. Then something else just as bewildering began to happen. I nipped my paw and said to myself: "Amazing the difference between town and country!"

I suddenly thought it really good not to have all those nasty cockroaches and beastly ticks, stupid cows around.

The rustic charm of the countryside attracts a lot of townees, I know. But I find the paths in the woods very uncomfortable. Fields and grass prick your paws and can't be compared with the lovely asphalt and tidy public parks of the town.

In all the better areas of town, you can carry on intelligent conversations with other fellows. In the country, you're constantly being forced into meeting rude horses, badly brought-up farm dogs and smelly cats.

At first I tried to show polite interest and be well-mannered, but then I became almost tearful. That's when I started longing to go back to the parks where I meet my friends.

Sometimes I wonder just who does decide things. It must be the Government. It can't very well be the master, as he gets so peculiar when the Government writes brown letters to him.

The master is a bit scared of the Government. He has been ever since he tried joking with them. It started with one of those brown letters. The Government, or to be more precise, the local Inland Revenue Department, wondered why the master had in all honesty and with clear conscience signed his tax declaration and forgotten to declare one item of income.

At first he turned scarlet with shame, then white with terror. "Must be those few coppers we got for me appearing in that magazine," I suggested consolingly. "Wasn't it *Sporting Dogs*?"

The master stiffened like a foxhound on the scent. "You're quite right, Freda. You're the one who earned the money, so they'll have to refer it to you . . . ha ha!" In a state of great excitement, the master wrote to the Government stating the correct factual circumstances.

To emphasize the importance of the statement, he made me sign it with a clear paw-mark, witnessed as genuine by his cackling friends.

At first the Government was struck dumb. Then the usual brown envelope arrived: ". . . as you state that you are a dog", etc., at which further clarification was requested.

I will be obedient if absolutely essential . . . but it doesn't take long for the mistress to succumb to the pleading in my eyes.

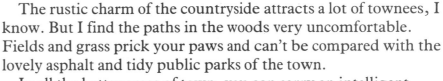

Chortling happily, the master clarified, and with rising anxiety, I had to put my paw-mark to it. I had a feeling the Government was not liking this one bit.

And I was right. Suddenly, the Government bared its fangs. The master was summoned to go round and see them. I thought the time had come to stop joking with the Government.

"Freda, I think you'd better go and see the Government now and explain yourself," the master said nervously.

Newly bathed and brushed, I was taken to the entrance hall of the Inland Revenue office, where debtors were scuttling back and forth looking for the right officials.

The master and I simultaneously caught sight of the notice. NO DOGS ALLOWED, it said.

Our profound respect for the law and all regulations forced us to leave the building immediately. The master wrote and explained why: ". . . I consider the prohibition of dogs in the Inland Revenue office must naturally be respected, just as I also realise that a neglectful taxpayer can hardly expect special treatment because she is a dog," he wrote in the letter, which I signed with my trembling law-abiding paw.

That shut the Government up. But then another brown letter came, addressed to me! ". . . in your capacity as a dog, you may delegate your responsibility to your Guardian, and request him promptly to adjust the tax due," the Government wrote.

I got away with nothing but a fright and a few bad dreams. But the master had a nasty supplementary tax demand.

One day, the master called out anxiously to me from the bathroom: "Tell me the truth now, Freda. Would you say I was beginning to put on weight a bit?"

"Yes, you are," I said. "Fat. Plump, to be exact." He gives me so much pleasure, I felt duty-bound at least to be honest.

But he wasn't at all pleased. He just sulked and walked nervously around with his stomach pulled in saying: "Fat? What do you mean, fat?"

Then I realized what kind of truth he'd wanted to hear. "We – ell, not fat exactly – slightly generously shaped here and there, you could say."

I should have said that, nice things, well-meaning, averting my eyes.

*Once a year I am examined by the family vet. He checks that
I'm fit and healthy – and not putting on too much weight as I
grow older.*

I can't make out this age business. At first I was far too young to understand. Then suddenly one is far too old to understand anything – when was one the right age?

They're the worst lies, as they mean the truth always has to be beautiful.

I am not eternally young. The fact of the matter is I'm now old. My nose had gone white, I move more slowly, see what I want to see and can still scent the good things in life. But I know what to expect. People probably don't.

121

One of the pleasures of ageing is remembering all the good intentions the master and mistress had when they first got me . . .

It's embarrassing to be old in today's society. You're greeted with such cries as: "I do believe old Freda thinks she's still a puppy!" I often hear that sort of rubbish. I want to nip them where it hurts them most – to play on their fear of Time.

When I was young, I was afraid of getting old, too. That's all part of youth, the undercurrent of our *joie de vivre*.

But you grow wiser with the years and understand better how to live your life. It's a matter of acting your age. You should be as old as you are and not what you'd like to be.

When a young puppy wants to grow big as soon as possible, it is a sign of guts and spirit.

But an old dog wanting to be young is to be pitied.

. . . I seem to remember one of the original ones being about no dogs being allowed on the sofa. Funny how no one notices now.

A taste of friendship

I'm going to tell you a little more about a dog I know. We meet almost every day. She lives in the neighbourhood. Even in the distance, she seems to be a merry little dot that's always bouncing about.

Her name is Scariff and she's an Irish setter. We've known each other for quite a while. I remember our first meeting – she came streaking along out of the dusk in the park. I liked her from her very first bark, and we ran round each other in huge circles all evening without having to say anything much.

I wondered for a long time what was so special about her and what it is that makes us seem so happy. How could I describe it?

I managed it in the end. Scariff is my closest friend.

I've pondered for years how to answer that exciting question – what is a friend? I haven't got a really good answer. There are so many answers. But there are not so many friends, when you come to think about it.

One probably knows quite a number at this stage, but that doesn't mean one's got lots of friends, only a great many acquaintances.

When you're young, you want to have lots of friends. It makes you feel very popular. When I grew a little older and wiser, I couldn't help noticing one thing – it is considered almost shameful not to have lots of friends.

"No wonder he hasn't a single friend," you hear people exclaiming about each other, in a truly spiteful way.

"I met someone yesterday who has become my best friend," I've often heard. Said by someone very young, of course.

To them I'd like to say that you don't make friends in the same way as you fetch a ball or a stick. One thing is quite clear – it takes time before an acquaintanceship develops into friendship.

Scariff is my best friend. We can run around or relax together without ever having to explain why.

Scariff looks very beautiful from every angle. Irish setters are much more elegant than golden retrievers.

Scariff isn't just any old Irish setter. Her name is the same as the place where her famous ancestors lived – Scariff. So Scariff isn't only a dog. She's also a small island off the tip of the south coast of Ireland.

That business of morally considering you have a whole island all to yourself caused Scariff some trouble at first. No one believed her, least of all me, for I've a healthy scepticism towards all boasters.

"Look for yourself then," barked Scariff, getting down the National Geographic's largest world atlas.

"So Chester ought to go round calling himself Newfoundland then?" I said teasingly, meaning Chester the Newfoundland who was born in Epping. Then Scariff almost flew at me, but in a friendly way, because of course it had to be the largest map in the world to show her silly little island, the size of a pinhead – a typical cause of bickering!

Friends do bicker like that. It's quite natural. When you daren't bicker a little – or drag in the world map for a joke – then you're only acquaintances. The question is – *when does one start bickering?* I would like to say that it's a question of time.

It takes time to make friends. No one can know beforehand just how long. It's like a new stick – you just don't know what it tastes like until you've chewed through the bark.

I think people take it much more lightheartedly. Their friends are like our sticks – something they chew on for a while, until they taste another stick.

The master has a tendency to come rushing home in an enthusiastic way every time he's made a new acquaintance.

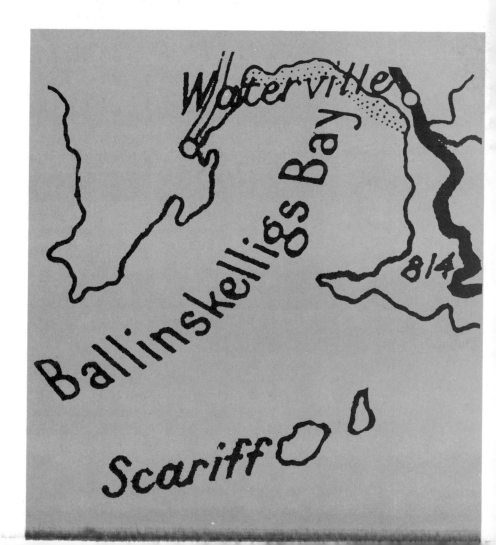

You know where you are with a friend, right down to the slightest nip and leap. I can trust Scariff.

"This one really is a friend you can rely on through thick and thin," he says, backed by his unerring knowledge of human nature.

When I crawl under the table, he asks me why I'm lying there looking snooty. "Because I suddenly thought of all the times you've later said . . . *and I thought that skunk was a real friend!*"

I also had to remind him that true friendship is a matter of scenting out its lasting qualities. Disappointment smells different, rather sour.

The great thing about the joy of reunion is that it is constantly repeated. We meet every day . . .

. . . and there's always a great deal of almost riotous fun as soon as we see each other.

Really true and lasting friendship always includes a special sort of joy – the joy of reunion, I mean.

Then there are a whole lot of other kinds of friendship – ranging from the master's eternal old school friends, and the mistress's friends at work, to the hordes of business-friends, golf-friends, art-friends, bridge-friends, poetry-friends, nature-friends and heaven knows what other sorts of friends who for some reason are called 'friends'.

Then I haven't even included the really large and important group of dog, cat, horse and other animal friends. But what I don't understand are people who are 'only friends' – "No, actually we're

There's probably a big difference between being 'girl-friends'
and being 'us boys together' friends. Women friends are
gentler, and kinder, I think.

only friends," they sigh, with heavy emphasis on the 'only'. They seem to refute a more profound friendship that way, especially if it's called love.

That 'only friends' sounds colder than 'unfriendly' or 'indifferent', at least that's what Scariff and I think. To be enemies demands involvement.

But anyone who stops being your friend never really was one in the first place. Just as you have to realise that you have to be friends before you can be enemies – and the other way round. I think friendship is something that's alive all the time. Friendship rises and falls like the lark trilling its evening song.

People have, of course, complicated all this with their different kinds of friendship. They maintain that real friendship only exists between men, strong types assuring each other in stifled voices and wobbling Adam's apples of their eternal friendship – as long as nothing unexpected crops up – though they never say that until the time comes.

Women are just *women friends*. That sounds nice, gentler somehow, and doesn't demand such a formal tone of voice.

We women friends offer each other small confidences that perhaps aren't always all that remarkable. So our friendship stays alive, like an inquisitive and snuffling nose.

I think there's something very moving about their friendship, even if Tom's hairs do tickle Patsy's mouth. Patsy is very protective and always watches over Tom.

Dog and cat

What I'm going to tell you now may require strong nerves, although it's about friendship.

Once again my friend Patsy is the focus of attention. By now, you know that Patsy is a typical canine specimen. You must also know that Tom is a typical feline. They see each other nearly every day. Patsy grabs Tom in her tremendously strong jaws.

First of all she scoops him up between her huge paws, then aiming at his skinny little neck, she shoves him in between her terrible canines and cautiously closes her jaws.

After that, Patsy strolls around for a while with Tom dangling from her mouth. He's big enough now to help a little with his hindlegs, which he likes doing. Dangling from Patsy's jaws, off goes Tom on his daily walk past the back door entrance.

Nearly every time they are disturbed by shrieking people: "Look . . . my God! That dog's killing the cat!"

Tom's mother, Sooty, is sitting on the gatepost watching the whole scene with her yellow eyes. She smiles wearily at the shouting people. "They're only dog and cat," she explains, to calm them down. But the people simply can't grasp it. When they talk about 'dog and cat', they mean exactly the opposite – snarling, fighting, clawing, scrapping.

This is all based on an unfortunate misunderstanding. When Tom wriggles with youthful impatience, Patsy carefully loosens her grip in order to be able to state what is important in this dog-cat relationship.

"You shouldn't draw the hasty conclusion that I like all cats. I just like this one cat in particular. As with dogs and people and creatures in general, my approval or disapproval is based on individuals. It is not possible to have an emotional relationship with a whole herd, or species, or breed."

Patsy thinks a dislike of cats, for instance, involves dangerous generalizations. Then, for instance, all white cats would consider they had the right to dislike all black cats. Dogs of one breed would harass dogs of another breed . . . that would lead to all kinds of craziness. Then the Reserve would be unbearable.

Loving one another

We quite often meet down in the meadow by the water. Then we really love each other, especially Pixie, the terrier, who is three. He tries to love practically everything that comes his way. Especially Patsy, who is four.

"Jolly nice doing something together," pants Pixie, while the good-natured Patsy takes on a rather more phlegmatic stance. Suddenly she sits down, and Pixie falls off in astonishment.

"I'm just waiting for Mister Right," Patsy explains, a slightly melancholy expression wrinkling her nose.

Pixie the terrier says nothing. He runs round for a while in the dewy meadow, looking quite free.

"Heave ho," he says, calmly climbing aboard Patsy, who girlishly sits down again. Pixie grows thoughtful, but doesn't give up that easily. He goes on loving her as hard as he can and the wind playfully ruffles their rumpled coats.

That's roughly what they got up to down there in the meadow.

In order to be good friends, it is important to be able to sniff at things together.

LEFT: *Pippa's friend Charlie, in my view a rather loutish Newfoundland, has taught her a lot of very silly things . . . but I let her try them out on me so that she'll have self-confidence when faced with fiercer situations.*

RIGHT: *And when I feel particularly generous, I'll let her win so that she can experience the triumph of victory.*

People say 'birds of a feather flock together', but that can't apply to Dad, the great dane, and little Patsy.

146

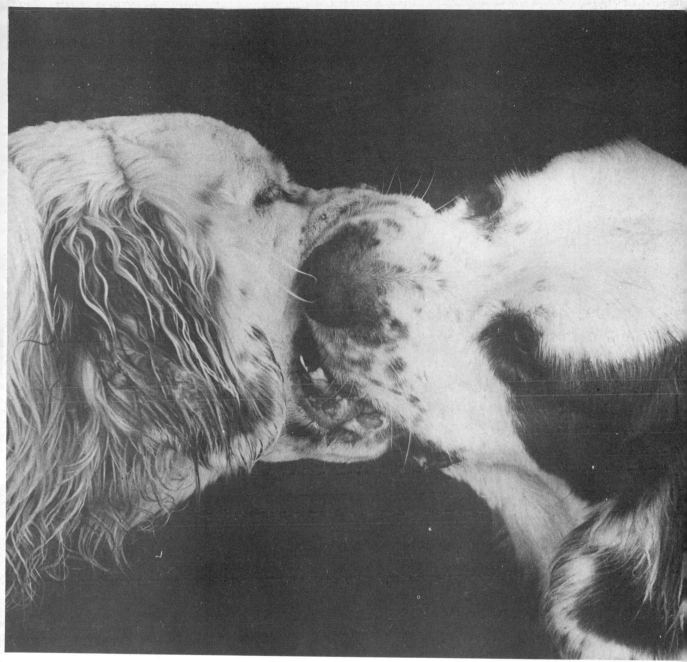

ABOVE: *This may look as if Patsy is trying to eat up her brother, Boots. But actually it's all just about a ball, and really quite affectionate.*

OPPOSITE: *We dogs usually think the best of each other, but we don't always see eye to eye. It takes a few cautious sniffs to establish good relations with a stranger.*

Who shakes my coat?

This is a very important question and I longed for an answer when I was down on the shore for the first time all by myself.

At home I was used to Mother Lisa doing most things. We preferred that when we were small. Then we didn't have to do anything that wasn't fun.

Suddenly there I was, soaking, newly dispatched into the world. I felt very miserable and unsafe in my dripping wet coat.

"What do I do now?" I anxiously asked Patsy and Nicky, the bearded collie.

"You do this!" explained Nicky, and shook himself. I copied him, shaking my coat just like Nicky.

That's roughly what it's like out in life. You learn by watching others.

Consequently I knew just what to say to Pippa when she complained in a rather spoilt and whiny way about water being horrible and wet.

She also splashed water right into the ears of morose old Butler, the basset, whose grave character condemns all forms of nonsense like playing with water. "Now, Pippa, would you please mind shaking yourself," he rumbled sternly.

Pippa shook herself, though somewhat incompetently. "There are certain things you can suddenly do all by yourself, as long as the will is there," I said, making quite sure she hadn't forgotten that last flip of the tip of her tail.

I mean the will to learn useful things. Useful things are mostly simple, but rather boring to learn. You have to keep your eyes open and see what other dogs do.

I first watched what Nicky did – then I did the same. It's not stealing ideas, but just attending the 'primary school of life'.

That's just why 'the others' are so useful. They do things you
yourself are not so good at, and you have to try to copy them and
learn.

But at the same time, you shouldn't always do exactly what
others do. It is the difference that takes some time to learn.

Fritz the dachshund is one of those who both likes and dislikes
the water. He was swimming marvellously and had funny little
bubbles in his beard until something suddenly occurred to him.

"Help!" shouted Fritz. "I can't swim. On second thoughts, I
think I'm bored by all this water." He happened to decide that just

as he was swimming past a small stone that looked very inviting,
sticking up right out of the water. Fritz climbed up onto it, and
stood there, thinking it rather restful, if somewhat disconcerting.

Dennis, a clever little border terrier who doesn't really like water but goes in anyway because he always needs to be the best, swam scornfully past Fritz, poised on his stone.

"You should get off before you fall in," cried Dennis, skilfully weaving his way past.

"I like it on this stone," Fritz answered calmly. "I've at last found my place in the world. It's just right here."

Fritz emphasizes that he's not at all scared, he's just enjoying such an excellent vantage point, and ignoring the chaos around him.

LEFT: *It's very strange, the
way that people look at Nature. I enjoy those peaceful
evenings by the river with the
mistress.*

RIGHT: *We are all part of
nature even if some of us do
seem alarmingly cold and
slippery.*

That's another thing only you can decide for yourself – when
things are *just right*. How great is the risk that you'll get your paws
wet? That's something everyone has to learn to decide.

Looking round the crowd at the lake, there are a lot of different
dogs here. Pippa is confused by all the different types of canines
she encounters, and can't believe there are even more varieties.

She bounces up and down excitedly. "Is it all of us down here on
the shore? How many others are there? Hundreds and hundreds?"

Not even I know how many we are. I just know that we are all
different. There must be a reason why pekinese are clearly so

No rabbit has ever caused me any annoyance, but there is nothing much to say about them.

different to great danes, although they are both dogs. And one must presume that a cat has different qualities to a horse – just as pekinese, great danes, labradors, bassets, cats and horses have their own characteristics.

Personally, I learnt fairly quickly how to differentiate between a

horse and a rabbit, but not everyone does. It isn't just because of size – it's the manner.

I'm grateful that rabbits don't behave like horses, and the other way round. It makes things easier and more predictable. That's why people are inclined to make convenient generalisations: southerners are cultivated, northerners are silent and hard-working . . .

But ever since I heard that my unbelievably talkative master is from the north, I have never ceased to be surprised that silence and industriousness are meant to be a northener's typical qualities.

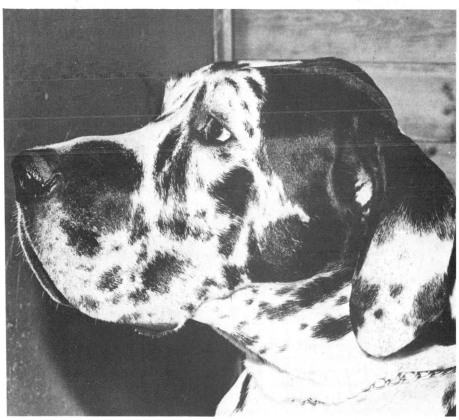

An imposing animal, the great dane is nothing at all to do with Denmark. A much feared fighting dog in Egypt, 4,000 years ago.

159

Man's oldest friend the horse, is gentle in spite of his size. But when you are small yourself, it is wise to keep your distance.

Borzoi, Russian greyhound, who lived on the steppes beyond Mongolia. The nobility's favourite as long as the nobility lasted. Now considered Beauty Number One.

The Afghan is an independent greyhound always apparently determined to escape. Even more independent is the Saluki, once a desert dog that hunted gazelle.

One thing I know about St Bernards is that they don't serve brandy in casks. But they save many people lost in the snows of the St Bernard Pass.

The Shetland sheepdog is a companion that, according to the experts, 'does not require much space'. I doubt that the sheep in the Shetland Isles thought that.

The English bloodhound is neither bloodthirsty, nor even English. It came from Normandy and has a leisurely temperament and a phenomenally keen scent.

Cheerful mixture of a Tibetan terrier and heaven knows what. This one lived on popcorn from the bars of Lebanon until it found a good home in England.

In nineteenth century England, the bull terrier fought bulls as popular entertainment. Then it was bred into a strong, all-white domestic dog.

The Komondor, a Hungarian breed that mustn't be washed. The dirt rattles off and settles in picturesque drifts in city apartments. Very exclusive.

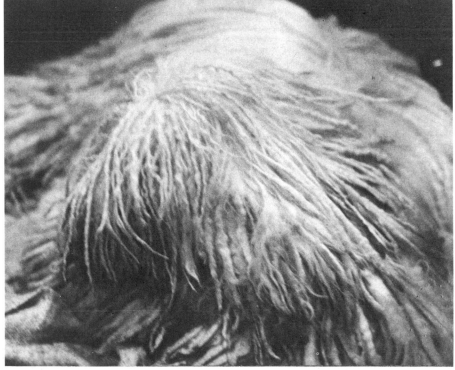

The Old English Sheepdog
looks like a small bear and
has a difficult coat to look
after. It can even be woven
into exquisite cloth.

The alsatian is the most popular breed in the world and
likes all climates. Marvellous
working dog. Has a reputa-
tion for being dangerous, but
they do have some dangerous
owners.

Italian greyhound, fine little fellow who trips his way through life. The Romans in antiquity kept it as a favourite, a miniature greyhound.

The bull mastiff was a popular fighting dog in Roman times and tore people to pieces. It's tame now and likes children, but is not a beginner's dog.

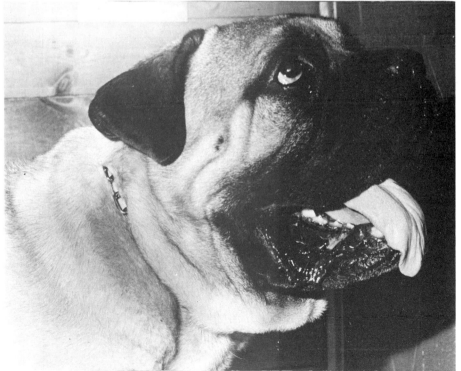

Japanese white pomeranian, lively barker with brilliant white coat that copes with mud and heat better than you would think. Stubborn, strong, happy and made in Japan.

Irish wolfhound, largest of all dogs, became almost extinct during the nineteenth century. It is considered incredibly good-natured, marvellous with children.

The bearded collie has guarded sheep since the Middle Ages, but was not admitted as a breed until 1964. Bright fellow with a coat that makes the master reach for the brush.

The basset artesien normand; French breed with good eyes. When it puts its nose to the ground, its ears hang over like a funnel and trap the scents inside – a popular cartoon animal.

Skye terrier, royal dog in 1842 when Queen Victoria acquired one. Appears good, but can be very obstinate, prefers being a one-man dog.

Poodle, or rather a 'large poodle'. Likes to see himself like a lion. Newly-clipped according to the regulations.

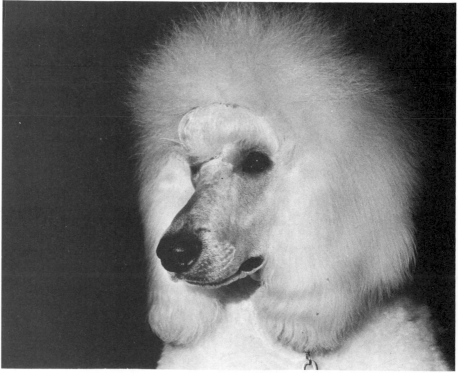

English mastiff. His powerful bite is not worth provoking. A family dog now, likes children though he used to fight bulls at fairgrounds.

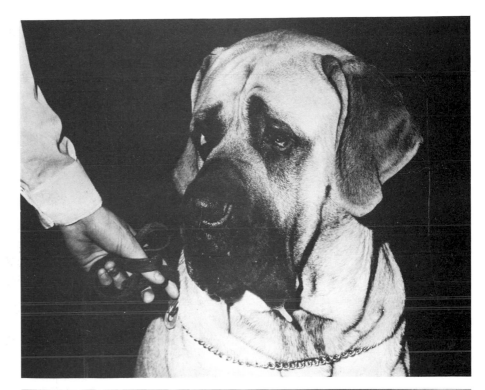

The dalmatian followed the gypsies in the eighteenth century and became 'top dog' in France. Chic too in England when a pair would often run alongside their master's carriage.

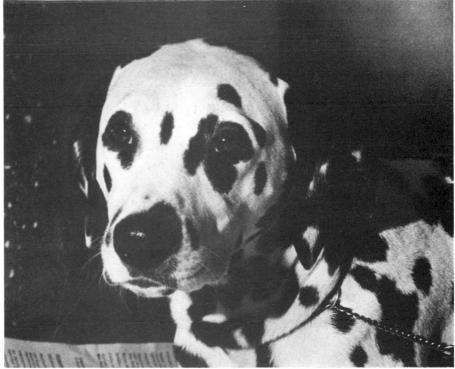

Friends for twelve thousand years

LEFT: *Our very differences in temperament mean that we enjoy each other's company.*

For thousands of years, we have welcomed people with pleasure and faithfully guarded their homes.

People may call us 'Man's best friend' but we weren't the first. The horse was first.

Their headstart is very noticeable. The horse originally helped people to survive, so the horse should hold the place of honour. We have also helped people. We track, carry, guard, protect – but we don't help them survive. Now its the reverse.

What do people really see in us? Once we were their feelers in dangerous terrains. We opened up the countryside to them, showed them what it was like, sharpened their instincts – perhaps even gave them a whiff of flight and freedom?

Then we became 'companions'. A 'companion' dog as a phenomenon goes back to the ruling classes of the past. In those

RIGHT: *We have always lain by their hearths ready and willing to give consolation and support.*

173

days, a rich man acquired a dog as a companion as proof of his wealth. The more useless the dog, the richer the man.

We were turned into beautiful objects to caress and to own.

Our only obligation now is to be slowly humanised, to have the right to be an animal taken away from us.

I once knew a quiet old pointer. He was promoted from being a hunting dog to being a 'member of the family'. He was allowed to sit at the dinner table and had his own bib.

He sat there year after year, growing obese, and his instincts slowly faded.

"Ruff's just like a human being!" boasted the pointer's mistress.

"Yes, you can teach him anything," his master exclaimed proudly. "Ruff's more clever than many people I know."

Things went well for years, until one fateful Sunday. During their traditional lunch of roast lamb and mint sauce, a little mouse suddenly appeared in the dining-room.

Ruff underwent a remarkable transformation. With a snarl, he hurled himself off his chair, raced under the table, his bib dangling, knocking his dish to the floor and causing an uproar.

Sometimes we can all get together without missing people. This gives us a pleasant feeling of independence – but we soon get hungry.

Lucas the alsatian believes it doesn't matter who steers just so long as you can trust them.

His master shouted and his mistress screamed. Right in front of their terrified eyes, the pointer caught the mouse and ate it as dessert.

At first they were going to have him put down – the pointer! Ruff had clearly become insane, gone quite mad and turned into a murderous hunting dog.

But he was allowed to live – although he had '*behaved like an animal*'.

That's one of the few stories I know about a dog who was obviously normal. All real dog stories are otherwise about the

amazing cleverness and human qualities of dogs.

I'm sure there isn't a single story about a really stupid dog! This is because in their goodness people want to pass on to us the qualities that they believe they possess.

So I fear that we are in danger of systematic 'humanisation' and that we will have our imperative right to be dogs taken away from us.

Liking animals has become a popular movement. Most people indulge in some kind of animal-liking. It's considered to be

Follow me! I don't know the way, but no doubt we'll find what we're looking for if we keep on going.

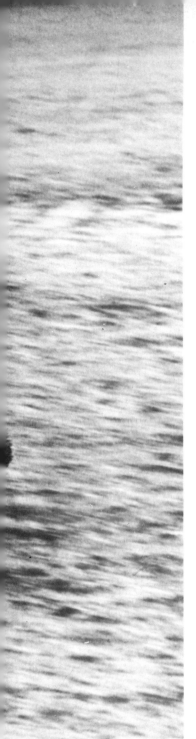

evidence of a gentle nature and general reliability.

I think it's good that people have us as domestic animals. Our instincts are still not yet quite blunted. We guide people to all the secret things found in the great outside. We teach them the scents of marshy plants, take them along forest paths and let them feel the whirling force of a flock of black grouse rising and making the whole world vibrate. We make it impossible for them to turn their backs on Nature.

There's a lot of lord-and-master nonsense that appears in well-known dog books such as the one I felt bound to chew up the other day.

For example, these dog manuals often have instructions as to how dogs should be patted. Patting should be 'encouragement for some task carried out'. So patting shouldn't happen only because you like each other and want to show it.

No, professional patting should occur 'when the dog pays attention to its owner's voice and rushes over to him, his tail wagging'.

But I believe patting should vary from dog to dog and person to person. All dogs like a pat now and then. It's up to each dog and his master to decide how much affection they should demonstrate to each other. It shouldn't be a reward system but a caring relationship.

Why do we chase after the same stick?

Suddenly Pippa is no longer an inquisitive little puppy.

She's an inquisitive young dog. She bustles about with her nose to the ground and her tail in the air. Her eyes have another kind of shine; they glow now with warm amber light, but still give out all the usual signals of mischief.

I myself have become whiter than ever round my grey nose. I'm no longer so lively, nor so inquisitive and restless.

I am quite content with Pippa's reports of what's going on in the great Reserve.

I receive her lively accounts in the seclusion of my corner, examining their content and telling her what they mean.

We may discuss something as simple as sticks. "Sticks taste of wood," says Pippa immediately, showing that the child in her is still there despite her seventy pounds.

"Sticks taste of Life itself," I say with dignity, meaning that if anyone knows that, I do.

I happen to have tasted thirteen thousand one hundred and forty sticks.

I wouldn't call it my favourite stick. It's just an ordinary stick but it's immensely chewable.

Pippa approaches every stick with a joy that is genuine, honest and uninhibited.

Good sticks certainly do not grow on trees

I have been amusing myself with some minor calculations. During my nine active years, I have chased after sticks for 3,285 working days.

If you discount certain idle days when I preferred to relax on the master's best sofa, I have allotted an average of four sticks to every active day, and that comes to 13,140 sticks that have passed through my mouth.

I am not stating this as a model achievement, or something that every dog should try to live up to. I am just indicating the frenzied central place stick-chasing has in every dog's life. And yet it seems as if it is one and the same stick we are chasing . . . a feeling, an instinct.

I don't wish to maintain there is anything remarkable about sticks. In fact, there is something humble about them, almost banal.

Sticks can be found more or less everywhere these days. They often look quite ordinary, somewhat straggly in appearance. It's easy to find them.

I usually roam round for a while with my nose to the ground until I find my first best stick. But I seldom get excited then. Sticks in themselves don't exactly produce the tingling anticipation of the unexpected. I usually calmly regard a stick as a strictly normal phenomenon in nature and maturely weigh up its quality and usefulness. This I decide with the help of routine sniffing, and if the aroma is right, I pick up the stick.

However, there now arises a rather interesting situation involving various alternatives:

I may, for instance, chew the stick. Or perhaps I may transform the stick into a little heap of splinters, something that often happens with young dogs in their undisciplined delight of chewing.

I usually choose the alternative of carrying the stick around with me for a while; for quite how long depends on the individual stick.

It won't actually be long before I find another stick. A stick with a fresher taste. A stick that sits better in the mouth. A stick that gives me a more varied shape.

Then I carry that stick around for a while until I happen to find the next stick, and after that the next one, after which I find another, until I suddenly see THE STICK! That is how your life flows by, stick by stick.

It really would be dreadful, though, if your life really did consist of nothing but a whole lot of sticks. A life should consist of a whole lot of emotions.

What I find most attractive about each stick is not the actual stick as such, *but that someone always wants to have it.* Someone tries to take my stick. In that way, sticks come alive. Then even the most rotten sticks become fun.

People laugh at Pippa when she sets off after sticks.

We are so childish. We keep on at it, sniffing after our sticks. We hunt sticks. We fight over sticks. We are absolutely beside ourselves with happiness when we find a good stick.

People say for heaven's sake, a stick's a stick . . . the whole world's full of sticks.

Then I say, call it something else apart from a 'stick'. Call it power, wealth, career, beauty, happiness or something else that is the most important thing in life for people. Turn it into a stick. Throw them away one after another . . . then you'll see.

I think I can say that it is not contented playfulness that characterises peoples' chasing after sticks.

"Fetch it, man!" He rushes straight off, jowls flapping and fangs flashing. The crunch comes when he manages to get his teeth into his stick. Ours have the fresher flavour of wood, I think.

One day when I was peacefully chewing a stick, Pippa came haring along like a black bundle of fur. I could see from a long way away what she wanted. She simply wanted to have my stick, and she bit into it firmly with a great snap.

It was one of those situations I'm sure most older dogs at once recognise. We are expected to drop the stick the moment a younger one comes and tugs at it.

*In a different mood, she approaches
Ziggy the Afghan who is making rash
claims on her stick.*

Pippa has now begun to grow into a good-natured but incurable stick-chewing labrador. She is so busy chewing that she hardly notices Ziggy's choreographic qualities until Ziggy insists that she joins in.

Gentle negotiations over a stick are carried on between a dog and a girl as a cautious game. But there is always a silent agreement that the dog will win as people rarely swim away with sticks in their mouths.

Pippa and I stood there in the meadow, tugging at the stick for a while until I thought things had gone far enough.

I gave her an indignant look, and may also have growled a little just to make my educational point quite clear. Pippa at once dropped the stick and loped off, whimpering feebly.

"Cheer up, Pippa. Life's full of sticks!" I called after her. "If you lose one, there's a thousand left," as they sing on the radio. Out of the corner of my eye, I saw that I was soon going to be proved right.

Zuri, a dashing cross between a labrador and a Rhodesian ridgeback, came tearing across the field. And what do you think she had in her mouth but a new stick.

When I saw Pippa and Zuri rushing off across the field in their swirling game, I sat down for a moment to have a slight think about this business of being old and young.

The struggle for sticks usually goes on all through life, but sometimes it's very easily solved. On the other hand, sometimes it's not!

ABOVE: *I, however, prefer to keep my sticks the easy way, by asserting seniority as soon as Pippa starts threatening to take my stick.*

OPPOSITE: *Zuri the mongrel is very successful at finding good sticks in unlikely places. Sometimes I think Zuri lets Pippa run off with sticks just for the excitement of a chase.*

A branch of reality

The stick must have been lying in all its scruffy decay in our meadow for a very long time.

Just how long, no one will ever know, but the bark had started flaking off, the juicy sap in the wood had dried out, and spots of mould had developed. In other words, it wasn't much of a stick. There were certainly better sticks, but I saw it first.

Just as I was about to pick the stick up in my careful, even dainty way, something extremely irritating happened. My chubby friend, Patsy, also happened to catch sight of a stick.

We may mean to give up our sticks generously, but actually it's sometimes easier just to share them.

Annoyingly enough, the stick she happened to catch sight of happened to be the stick that I actually saw first. Naturally I considered that it was *mine*.

So there we were in the meadow in a situation that on my part I think is extremely embarrassing, almost painful. We had both taken a firm grip on the same stick. There was a slight crunching of rotten wood and bits of bark flaked off as we pulled and tugged in each direction.

I had no wish to be too brusque. I wished to give Patsy a chance to hand over my stick in a spirit of generosity, but unfortunately she seemed to be of another opinion. She tugged irritably at what she clearly regarded as *her* stick, at the same time looking very offended.

It was one of those marvellous early spring days, the air fresh and clear and obviously easy to breathe. But there was something thick and suffocating constricting my throat. I felt quite definitely that something was about to happen. There was a kind of thumping going on inside me called *rage*.

Patsy also seemed to be afflicted with a similar breathlessness.

Her grip on my stick hardened as subdued wheezes came from her chubby body. A hard gleam set in her eyes and white froth appeared at the corners of her mouth, which is usually at such a cheerful angle.

Every stick has its 'moment of truth' when you hope that the other one will give way.

Now it was twisted into a grimace of avarice from her desire for my stick.

Patsy lost her general good nature and began to snarl – just because of a silly stick! This remarkable transformation forced my attention to waver for the second it took her to wrench my stick away.

When Patsy shuts her jaws, it sounds like a carboot closing. In that boot was my stick! The story should end there.

OPPOSITE: *Who has the stick doesn't matter – as long as it isn't the other one!*

But it didn't. You might almost say that it started there. Patsy lolloped off with my stick and with me chasing her. You could say that its a minor fundamental situation everyone knows about – not only dogs!

Everyone is chasing after something someone else has got. The chase is sometimes more important than what we're after. There's a plentiful supply of sticks. To maintain 'sticks don't grow on trees' I call a rather hasty conclusion. There are so many sticks, that according to the most elementary principles of sharing, there ought to be enough for us all.

BELOW: *Now I've taken the tactical inner track, I'm an expert in taking tight corners, but Patsy is more worried about Nicky's advance.*

But unfortunately it is not like that – because someone else always has the particular stick you regard as yours. This could also be the answer to the eternal question – *why do we chase after the same stick?*

There is a short-lived alliance between me and Patsy as we both tackle Nicky – and he pants and sweats inside his thick coat, as he makes the mistake of heading for the cool water.

If you study people playing together, you can see quite clearly that what they're really doing is fighting playfully. They compare, measuring up each other's strength and looking for gaps in each other's defences. Someone wins. Someone else loses.

I always go out when the master loses at 'Pick-A-Stick' against the mistress! Their games with sticks involve far too great an element of competitiveness, which makes them sharp-tempered and kills the actual desire to play.

"Ah, my dear sticks, you who scratch our tongues but give our lives its harsh sweetness!" as Butler the basset puts it, as his short legs and long ears don't allow much active participation in stick-hunting.

I think that's a very poignant observation, a good image of the role of sticks in our lives.

All labradors and retrievers come into their own in the water, but Patsy takes no notice. She may be heavy and chubby on land but in the water, weighing less, she is much more mobile.

In a spirit of generosity, I appeared to hand my place in the hunting team over to Nicky, the bearded collie. He hared off after Patsy and my stick, his eyes wild and his coat billowing.

But I am not entirely as noble as that. The water was glittering in the distance. It's always part of my tactics to drive stick-hunts towards the water, for once there I know rivals like the long-haired Nicky will simply become soaking-wet clodhoppers.

Unsuspecting, the dogs raced out into the water. Calmly, I followed and carefully removed the stick from the panting Patsy. With that, I felt the matter was at an end.

Now perhaps it appears that things are somewhat heated between Patsy and me, and I assure you this has been nothing but a game all along. In addition, the water cools us down.

We may seem to be what they call 'stick-crazy' in expert circles. Modern dog books disapprove of sticks, which 'may lead to reckless rivalries'.

ABOVE: *The stick-hunt suddenly becomes more serious, growls and snarls all round and total concentration so that we may even look rather dangerous.*

I must tell you about one who really was stick-crazy. He had a thick green cloth coat, a shaving-brush sticking out of his hat, a Shooting Club gold medal and a chocolate brown labrador.

They came to our bathing place. In harsh tones, Shaving-brush ordered our masters and mistresses to stand aside, as he was going to practise what he called 'advanced retrieval techniques' with his labrador.

"Fetch it!" roared Shaving-brush and started chucking a whole lot of things into the water. "I'm de-fixating the dog from definite objects," he explained to all of us idiots standing around.

Naturally this labrador felt no particular sympathy with all those things his master was hurling into the water – sticks, beer-cans, a disgusting old plastic bag, a bit of bicycle tyre, an apple core, a crumpled cigarette pack, a soaking wet telephone directory – everything mankind in his energy-wasting love of nature can't be bothered to put into rubbish bins and skips.

But the labrador loyally toiled back and forth, in and out of the water, salvaging all that garbage. "Now we'll see how advanced retrieval techniques really come into their own when the dog is properly trained and used to obeying its owner," explained Shaving-brush.

OPPOSITE: *We know we are just as strong as each other – If we weren't, the game would never get this far.*

The struggle continues. Then suddenly I feel something wooden in my mouth – the stick! Patsy decides to rest and regain her strength.

"Fetch it!" he roared, hurling his elegant walking-stick with a silver crook into the water. Then both Patsy and I saw the same thing – a definite gleam in the labrador's eye, a glint of collusion between us dogs.

At first the labrador sat down as if glued to the sand. Then he lay down with a tiny sigh and rather absently started licking his paws. He stared faithfully at his master, but appeared to be totally deaf and blind to the walking-stick, now bobbing up and down a long way out from the shore.

"Fetch it! For Christ's sake, fetch it!" bellowed Shaving-brush.

The labrador calmly went on licking himself and then rose and listlessly watered a nearby bush.

It was a battle of wills. But as Shaving-brush had remarked, the labrador has a 'steady psyche'. So, swearing terribly, his master had to roll up his hunting-green trouser legs and start wading out towards the bobbing stick, which did actually have a genuine silver crook.

He had to swim the last bit. But his magnificently drilled labrador stood on the shore wagging his tail encouragingly.

Playful little exercises like that get the master out of the silly

habit of persistently throwing sticks in that foolish way, both Patsy and I thought we saw his yellow eyes saying.

But he didn't say it. Anyhow, that would be laying it on a bit thick in this long story.

Every story about every stick usually ends in one way. Roughly like this: someone at last succeeds in getting hold of the stick, the ultimate aim of stick-hunting.

The someone on this occasion is me! I savour the bark of the stick and the sweetness of victory.

But something terrible might happen: "You just take the stick while I have a rest," Patsy might say if she were feeling piqued. That's the worst thing you can say during stick-hunting. Even the best stick loses its flavour after a remark like that.

So Patsy says nothing. She encourages me with her melancholy look of defeat. There's nothing like the fatigue after the chase – colours and scents return and merge gently into each other.

That's when Life tastes of nothing but stick.

Poodle at large

We are both just beginning to tire of the stick when we suddenly become aware of something. A poodle, to be more precise.

With an obvious aim in mind, he comes swaggering along the shore, then stops in a casually amused pose and says with a self-satisfied laugh: "Hey, you two little squirts . . . give over splashing now and sling over the stick."

Unfortunately I can't reproduce his actual tone of voice and that grating sound when a supercilious poodle laughs. But I can tell you it is very annoying, even infuriating.

"Little girls shouldn't mess about fighting over sticks. Little girls should just be pretty," the poodle laughs, backing away from our splashing.

I can feel my coat beginning to crawl and I can see Patsy's upper

When the poodle tries to talk his way in, I turn very suspicious and nasty.

I know that intellectuals are afraid of violence. I saw that on the video of Jaws.

lip curling slightly, as if she were taking the safety-catch off her canines. Just as I am about to give the poodle a sharp rebuke, I remember Conrad.

Conrad was also a poodle, but he thought he was more than that. He believed himself superior to the rest of us and had an irritatingly high tail stance. He was always telling me how clever he was, how much praise he always got, and that he had a hand-made basket with a Scottish plaid rug in it.

212

Conrad kept telling us that his master had 'contacts in high places', and his mistress had a fur coat from Paris. Conrad reckoned he was no ordinary dog. He was more with it. He belonged to the chosen few and 'was going places in the world'.

I suppose that was even grander than lying on a Scottish plaid rug in a hand-made basket, but we didn't really know what Conrad meant.

Anyhow, the whole pack thought he was fairly ghastly. I thought Conrad seemed to be lonely more than anything else.

Conrad was always saying how important it was to be 'with it'. "You have to keep in with the chosen in the Reserve, with the élite. You have to pick out the best sticks."

"I just want power," he said. "I want power and responsibility, and to make decisions for others in the Reserve." We laughed ourselves silly.

Conrad was not especially quick. He was definitely not strong, but actually rather good at handing out little nips from behind. "But others do the same," he said indignantly, when we scolded him, saying he made a poor friend.

Conrad though himself rather smart. "You always have to be smart and make the most of opportunities," he said with a wry grin. He had learnt that at home from his master, who had 'contacts in high places'.

Were they birds? No, 'contacts in high places' were people who had power, Conrad explained. They made decisions for the little men and the 'grassroots' – "That's you lot, that is."

We soon grew tired of Conrad and chased him away. He raced off, yelping, in pursuance of his career.

Funny how little they understand, and how much they need us.
It is a good life. They may not supply many sticks but they give
us most things we want, including friendship.

But where have all the sticks gone?

This is a matter increasingly being pushed into the background.

You take sticks for granted. They should always be there in front of your nose, ready to be picked up or abandoned for some other stick that tastes better.

You relate to sticks as to the rest of life.

Now I ought to answer that question – Well, Freda, which were your best sticks?

Answer – I don't know. I simply don't know, because every good life is lined with so many different sticks. They all have a definite flavour of wood. Sometimes you enjoy the exciting aroma of success, but usually it's the salt of the struggle or the bitter taste of defeat.

My best sticks have the silky taste of friendship.

This book has been mostly about those sticks.

"But supposing people thought friendship was not very exciting to read about?" asks Pippa uneasily.

She says nothing much happens in my world. Too few thrills. Not much action. Well, I think that's a good life.

Nothing exciting has to happen. Good days are rarely fantastic, nor even good weather. They are just good.

"Pippa, if you just turn over the page, I'll show you a picture of what I mean by a good life."

Where do all the sticks go?

They disappear, however carefully you chew.

But friendship never does that.